Made from scratch

EVERYDAY
EASY
HOME
COOKING

This edition published by Parragon Books Ltd in 2014 and distributed by
Parragon Inc.
440 Park Avenue South, 13th Floor
New York, NY 10016
www.parragon.com/lovefood

LOVE FOOD is an imprint of Parragon Books Ltd

ISBN 978-1-4723-2998-1

Printed in China

Cover photography by Ian Garlick
Design by Geoff Borin
New photography by Clive Streeter
New recipes, introduction and notes by Rachel Carter
Nutritional analysis by Fiona Hunter

Notes for the Reader
This book uses standard kitchen measuring spoons and cups. All spoon and cup
measurements are level unless otherwise indicated. Unless otherwise stated,
milk is assumed to be whole, eggs are large, individual vegetables are medium,
and pepper is freshly ground black pepper. Unless otherwise stated, all root
vegetables should be peeled prior to using.

Garnishes, decorations and serving suggestions are all optional and not
necessarily included in the recipe ingredients or method. Any optional
ingredients and seasoning to taste are not included in the nutritional analysis.
The times given are an approximate guide only. Preparation times differ
according to the techniques used by different people and the cooking times
may also vary from those given. Optional ingredients, variations or serving
suggestions have not been included in the time calculations.

Contents

Introduction 4

Speedy Soups 6

Healthy Soups 36

Hearty Soups 66

Around the World 96

Index 126

Introduction

Whether you need a comforting winter warmer, a light summer bite, or a quick and easy weeknight dinner—soup is the ideal solution to mealtime dilemmas. Easy to make, great for leftovers, and packed with nutritious ingredients, it's a filling and endlessly adaptable part of any cook's repertoire.

Few dishes are as versatile as soup: they are an economical way of using cupboard staples and leftover foods, and they are often a quick, fuss-free me that can be made with ease. Soup can also be a simple way to include health boosting ingredients in your diet. Packed with vegetables, and often low in saturated fat, they are a good go-to meal whether you're watching your weig or not. Plus, with the addition of grains, beans, pastas, and noodles, soup is a great way to stay fuller for longer, keeping hunger pangs at bay with these added carbohydrates.

Soups can be served as a palate cleanser before a big meal, or between courses, as a light appetizer before a rich main dish or as a substantial meal in a bowl all by itself. They are great for lunch and serve as the ideal midday energy booster.

The chapters of this book include Speedy Soups, which contains recipes that are ready to go in under an hour, and require a minimal amount of pre-cooking preparation. Healthy Soups are ideal for anyone keeping an eye on their food intake, as all the recipes are low in calories or saturated fat but still packed with ingredients to keep you satisfied. Hearty Soups includes substantial meal-in-a-bowl soups with pasta and pulses. There are also some classic puréed soups containing root vegetables and squashes, which are at their best in the colder months. The Around the World chapter has a selectio of some of the best international soup recipes.

With minimal ingredients, prep and a simple on-the-hob cooking process, soups are a good fuss-free meal full of nutrients to slot into busy lifestyles.

The Essential Staples

• Basic Vegetables

Onions, (try buying them diced and frozen, to save yourself time), garlic, and ginger (which are also available in long-life jars or frozen), celery, leeks, and carrots are all ideal for making a flavorful base for soup.

• Prepared Stock

There is a huge variety of stock options readily available from the supermarket—there are cartons and cans of liquid stock, dried bouillon cubes, packets and jars of dried stock powder, and jars of stock base. Keep a

selection in different flavors, if you can, but chicken bouillon cubes and vegetable bouillon cubes are definite pantry essentials.

• Oils

There is no need to use expensive extra virgin olive oil in soup. A basic canola, olive, or vegetable oil with a neutral flavor is preferable.

• Flavorings

Keep good-quality sea salt and whole black peppercorns, because these provide a good depth of flavor. Other basic condiments that often come in useful include balsamic vinegar, tomato paste, dark soy sauce, miso paste, mustard (French and whole-grain), ketchup, and Worcestershire sauce. There are also an increasing assortment of pastes available, and those with Parmesan and dried porcini mushrooms provide a hit of flavor that complements both vegetable- and meat-base soups.

• Beans

Whether you choose dried or canned beans, they should always be on hand because they add bulk and flavor and are both nutritious and easy on the budget. Remember that not all dried beans need to be soaked before using— split peas, red lentils, and adzuki beans can be added directly to the soup after a quick rinse in cold water. Dried red lentils can be cooked in the soup, along with other ingredients without the need for soaking, and because they are high in protein, they are ideal for

adding to vegetable soups. Keep a small selection of canned beans, such as cranberry, cannellini, red kidney beans, black beans, chickpeas, and lima beans as a standby for bulking out hearty soups in the winter months.

• Dried Herbs & Spices

A well-stocked pantry with dried spices should include smoked paprika, curry powder, cumin seeds, ground coriander, cumin, dried chiles or crushed red pepper flakes, and black peppercorns. Woody herbs, such as rosemary, thyme, and oregano, retain their flavor well in a dried format, but leafy herbs, such as cilantro, basil, and parsley, are best used fresh.

• Canned Ingredients

Canned tomatoes are an essential item on the weekly shop list, and these are available with extra flavorings, such as basil and garlic, which can save time. Jars or cans of sun-dried tomatoes in olive oil, roasted peppers, olives, capers, pesto, and anchovies are also useful to keep at home.

• Dried Pasta & Noodles

Dried soup pasta and most noodles are an ideal addition to soups (especially broths). You can also use regular dried pasta, but this takes longer to cook. Both pasta and noodles are handy because they have a long shelf life and a neutral flavor that goes well with stronger soups.

Tomato Soup *8*

Leek & Potato Soup *10*

Pea Soup *12*

Fishermen's Soup *14*

Chilled Avocado Soup *16*

Ham & Lentil Soup *18*

Lemon, Chicken, & Rice Soup *20*

Carrot & Parsnip Soup *22*

Bean Soup *24*

Cabbage & Bacon Soup *26*

Spicy Corn Chowder *28*

Chicken & Chipotle Soup *30*

Mixed Squash Soup *32*

Spicy Chicken Noodle Soup *34*

Speedy Soups

Tomato Soup

nutritional information per serving	100 cal, 6g fat, 0.8g sat fat, 5.5g total sugars, 0.4g salt

This soup is ready in minutes and made with pantry ingredients, perfect for a warming lunch or a quick appetizer.

INGREDIENTS

2 tablespoons olive oil

1 large onion, chopped

1 (14½-ounce) can whole plum tomatoes

1¼ cups vegetable stock

1 tablespoon tomato paste

1 teaspoon hot pepper sauce

handful of fresh basil leaves

salt and pepper, to taste

1. Heat the oil in a large saucepan over medium heat, then add the onion and sauté for 4–5 minutes, stirring, until soft. Add the tomatoes, stock, tomato paste, hot pepper sauce, and half the basil leaves.

2. Process using a handheld immersion blender until smooth. Stir the soup over medium heat until just boiling, then season with salt and pepper.

3. Serve the soup in warm serving bowls, garnished with the remaining basil leaves.

GOES WELL WITH Toasted wholemeal bread and grated mature Cheddar cheese

Leek & Potato Soup

SERVES 6

PREP TIME:
15 minutes

COOKING TIME:
20–25 minutes

nutritional information
per serving — 195 cal, 13g fat, 8g sat fat, 3g total sugars, 0.6g salt

This soup has a velvety texture and mild flavor that makes it wonderful for warming you up in the depths of winter—which is especially good, because this is when leeks are at their best flavor and price.

INGREDIENTS

4 tablespoons butter
1 onion, chopped
3 leeks, sliced
2 Yukon gold, red-skinned,
or white round potatoes,
cut into ¾-inch cubes
3½ cups vegetable stock
salt and pepper, to taste
⅔ cup light cream, to serve
snipped fresh chives,
to garnish

1. Melt the butter in a large saucepan over medium heat, add the onion, leeks, and potatoes, and sauté gently for 2–3 minutes, until soft but not brown. Pour in the stock, bring to a boil, then reduce the heat and simmer, covered, for 15 minutes.

2. Process using a handheld immersion blender, until smooth.

3. Heat the soup gently and season with salt and pepper. Ladle into warm bowls, garnish with a swirl of cream and snipped chives, and serve immediately.

1

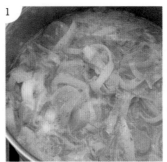

1

2

FREEZING TIP
This soup is great
to have as a freezer
standby. Chill after
cooking and pour into
an airtight container or
a large pitcher lined
with a plastic food
bag. Seal and freeze
for up to three months.

Pea Soup

nutritional information per serving	274 cal, 16g fat, 10g sat fat, 3.5g total sugars, 0.9g salt

Peas are the essence of summer, and their sweet flavor works well in soup. Topped with crumbled Roquefort and crispy croutons, this is a mouthwatering delight.

INGREDIENTS

3 tablespoons butter
¼ cup finely chopped shallots
4 cups vegetable stock or water
3 cups shelled peas
pinch of sugar
¼ cup crème fraîche
or Greek yogurt
salt and pepper, to taste
croutons and blue cheese,
such as Roquefort, crumbled,
to serve

1. Melt the butter in a large saucepan over medium heat. Add the shallots and sauté for 2–3 minutes, or until soft. Add the stock, peas, and sugar, season with salt and pepper, and bring to a boil, uncovered. Simmer for 15–20 minutes, or until the peas are tender.

2. Strain the peas and reserve the cooking liquid. Process the peas in a food processor or blender, until smooth, then return the puree to the pan. Gradually stir in the cooking liquid until you have the desired consistency.

3. Reheat the soup; do not boil. Stir in the crème fraîche or yogurt and adjust the seasoning, if necessary. Serve immediately with blue cheese and croutons sprinkled over the soup.

COOK'S NOTE
Use either frozen
or freshly
shelled peas in
this recipe. If
preferred, swap
the Roquefort
for a milder
blue cheese,
such as Stilton.

Fishermen's Soup

 SERVES 6   PREP TIME: 10 minutes   COOKING TIME: 20–25 minutes

nutritional information per serving	333 cal, 20g fat, 3g sat fat, 4g total sugars, 0.3g salt

Use your own choice of firm white fish—teamed with crusty bread, this soup makes a quick, complete meal.

INGREDIENTS

2 pounds mixed white fish, such as cod, halibut, red snapper, and sea bass, and peeled shrimp

⅔ cup olive oil

2 large onions, sliced

2 stalks celery, thinly sliced

2 cloves garlic, chopped

⅔ cup white wine

4 tomatoes, chopped

pared rind of 1 orange

1 teaspoon chopped fresh thyme

2 tablespoons chopped fresh parsley

2 bay leaves

salt and pepper, to taste

croutons and lemon wedges, to serve

1. Cut the fish into large portions, discarding any skin. Heat the oil in a saucepan, add the onion, celery, and garlic, and sauté for 5 minutes, or until softened.

2. Add the fish and shrimp to the pan, then add the wine, tomatoes, orange rind, herbs, and bay leaf. Season with salt and pepper and add enough cold water to cover. Bring to a boil, then simmer, uncovered, for 15 minutes, or until the fish is cooked through and flakes easily.

3. Remove and discard the bay leaf. Ladle into warm bowls and serve immediately, with croutons and lemon wedges.

Chilled Avocado Soup

 SERVES 4

 PREP TIME:
10 minutes
plus chilling

 COOKING TIME:
No cooking

nutritional information
per serving   311 cal, 29g fat, 12g sat fat, 2g total sugars, 0.4g salt

On a hot day, this soup makes the perfect appetizer for a refreshing summer meal. Serve thoroughly chilled.

INGREDIENTS

2 avocados

1 tablespoon lemon juice

1 tablespoon snipped fresh chives, plus extra to garnish

1 tablespoon chopped fresh flat-leaf parsley

2 cups chicken stock, chilled

1¼ cups light cream, plus extra to serve

dash of Worcestershire sauce

salt and pepper, to taste

1. Halve the avocados and remove the pits. Scoop out the flesh and coarsely chop.

2. Put the avocado flesh, lemon juice, chives, parsley, stock, cream, and Worcestershire sauce in the blender and process until smooth. Season with salt and pepper.

3. Transfer the soup to a bowl, cover, and chill until required. Serve with light cream drizzled over the soup, topped with snipped chives.

1

2

3

COOK'S NOTE
The soup is best consumed within a couple of hours of making and is delicious served with seafood, such as crab or shrimp.

Ham & Lentil Soup

 SERVES 2   PREP TIME:
10 minutes    COOKING TIME:
25–30 minutes

nutritional information per serving	374 cal, 11.5g fat, 2.5g sat fat, 5.5g total sugars, 3.5g salt

Transform cold, cooked ham into a healthy, hearty winter meal packed with goodness that will leave you feeling full and contented.

INGREDIENTS

8 ounces cooked ham

1 tablespoon vegetable oil

1 onion, finely chopped

1 clove garlic, finely chopped

1 carrot, finely diced

1 celery stalk, thinly sliced

1 (15-ounce) can green lentils, drained

1 teaspoon finely chopped fresh rosemary leaves,

2½ cups vegetable stock or ham stock

pepper, to taste

1. Using two forks, finely shred the cooked ham and set aside.

2. Heat the oil in a saucepan over medium–high heat. Add the onion, garlic, carrot, and celery and sauté for 4–5 minutes, or until starting to soften.

3. Add the lentils, rosemary, shredded ham, and stock, and season with pepper. Cover and simmer for 20 minutes, or until the vegetables are just tender. Serve immediately.

1

2

3

FREEZING TIP
Freeze for up to
six months in an
airtight container.
Defrost completely
and reheat to serve.

Lemon, Chicken, & Rice Soup

SERVES 4

PREP TIME:
10 minutes

COOKING TIME:
15–20 minutes

nutritional information
per serving | 341 cal, 6.5g fat, 1.5g sat fat, 3g total sugars, 0.9g salt

This soup is packed with fresh flavors—lifted by a zingy dose of lemon juice.

INGREDIENTS

1 tablespoon vegetable oil
1 onion, finely chopped
1 leek, finely chopped
1 clove garlic, crushed
finely grated zest and
juice of ½ lemon
½ cup long-grain rice
4 cups chicken stock
2 cooked chicken breasts,
coarsely chopped
3½ cups fresh spinach
1 cup frozen peas
¼ cup chopped fresh
flat-leaf parsley
salt and pepper, to taste
Parmesan cheese, to serve

1. Heat the oil in a large saucepan over medium heat. Sauté the onion and leek for 4–5 minutes, until starting to soften. Add the garlic and lemon zest and cook for an additional 1–2 minutes.

2. Add the rice and stock and bring to a boil. Cover and simmer for 8 minutes. Add the chicken, spinach, and peas and season with salt and pepper. Cook for an additional 4 minutes, until the rice is cooked through.

3. Stir in the lemon juice and parsley and serve with some Parmesan cheese shavings sprinkled on top.

1

2

3

COOK'S NOTE
Only add the lemon juice when you are just about to serve the soup, otherwise it will cause the green vegetables to lose their color.

Carrot & Parsnip Soup

SERVES 6   PREP TIME: 10 minutes   COOKING TIME: 30–35 minutes

nutritional information per serving	92 cal, 1g fat, 0.2g sat fat, 8g total sugars, 0.4g salt

Carrots and parsnips are both naturally sweet, and they work together well in soup. The chervil's flavor adds a delicious freshness to this light and simple recipe.

INGREDIENTS

6 carrots, chopped
3 parsnips, chopped
4 shallots, chopped
4 fresh chervil sprigs
3½ cups vegetable stock
salt and pepper, to taste
heavy cream, to garnish

1. Put the carrots, parsnips, shallots, and chervil into a saucepan, pour in the stock, and season with salt and pepper. Bring to a boil, reduce the heat, and simmer for 20–25 minutes, until the vegetables are tender.

2. Remove the pan from the heat and let cool slightly. Remove and discard the chervil, then transfer to a food processor or blender, in batches if necessary, and process until smooth.

3. Return the soup to the rinsed-out pan and reheat gently; do not boil. Ladle into warm bowls, swirl about 1 tablespoon of cream on the top of each, and serve.

1

2

3

COOK'S NOTE
If you prefer, don't peel the carrots and parsnips—a quick scrub will be enough.

Bean Soup

 SERVES 6   PREP TIME: 5 minutes    COOKING TIME: 25–30 minutes

nutritional information per serving	270 cal, 8g fat, 1.5g sat fat, 0.5g total sugars, 0.3g salt

Here is a fantastic staples recipe that is ready in minutes, with virtually no preparation necessary.

INGREDIENTS

1¼ cups drained and rinsed canned cannellini beans

1¼ cups drained and rinsed canned cranberry beans

about 2½ cups chicken stock or vegetable stock

4 ounces dried soup pasta

¼ cup olive oil

2 garlic cloves, minced

3 tablespoons chopped fresh flat-leaf parsley

salt and pepper, to taste

1. Put half the cannellini beans and half the cranberry beans in a food processor or blender with half the stock and process until smooth. Pour into a large saucepan and add the remaining beans. Stir in enough of the remaining stock to achieve the desired consistency, then bring to a boil.

2. Add the pasta and return to a boil, then reduce the heat and cook for 15 minutes, or until just tender.

3. Meanwhile, heat 3 tablespoons of the oil in a small skillet. Add the garlic and cook, stirring continuously, for 2–3 minutes, or until golden. Stir the garlic into the soup with the parsley.

4. Season with salt and pepper and ladle into warm bowls. Drizzle with the remaining oil and serve immediately.

1
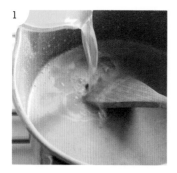

2

3

Cabbage & Bacon Soup

nutritional information per serving	330 cal, 18.5g fat, 6g sat faat, 8.5g total sugars, 2.9g salt

A flavorsome soup that packs a punch—perfect served with warm tear-and-share bread or some crispy croutons.

INGREDIENTS

1 tablespoon vegetable oil
2 cloves garlic, crushed
1 onion, peeled and finely chopped
2 celery stalks, chopped
8 ounces smoked bacon, chopped
1 savoy cabbage, cored and shredded
5½ cups chicken stock
1 teaspoon Worcestershire sauce
pepper, to taste
2 tablespoons chopped fresh flat-leaf parsley, to serve

1. Heat the oil in a large skillet over medium–high heat. Add the garlic, onion, and celery and sauté for 4–5 minutes, or until softened.

2. Add the bacon and sauté for an additional 3–4 minutes, or until starting to brown.

3. Add the cabbage, stock, and Worcestershire sauce and season with pepper. Cover and simmer for 15–20 minutes.

4. Process in a blender or food processor until smooth. Serve with the parsley sprinkled over the soup.

2

3

4

Spicy Corn Chowder

 SERVES 6   PREP TIME: 15 minutes    COOKING TIME: 30–35 minutes

nutritional information per serving	188 cal, 5.5g fat, 0.8g sat fat, 6.5g total sugars, 0.5g salt

An unusual twist on a classic chowder, in this recipe silken tofu is pureed to add a creamy texture, which complements the vegetables and fresh herbs.

INGREDIENTS

1 tablespoon olive oil

1 onion, diced

2 cloves garlic, finely chopped

2 carrots, diced

2 celery stalks, diced

1 red bell pepper, seeded and diced

3 cups frozen corn kernels

½ teaspoon chili powder

4 cups vegetable stock

8 ounces silken tofu, drained

2 tablespoons chopped cilantro, to garnish

3 scallions, thinly sliced, to garnish

1. Heat the oil in a large skillet over medium–high heat. Add the onion and garlic and cook, stirring occasionally, for about 5 minutes, or until soft.

2. Add the carrots, celery, bell pepper, corn, chili powder, and stock. Bring to a boil, reduce the heat to medium–low, and simmer, uncovered, for about 20 minutes, or until the vegetables are soft.

3. Process the tofu along with a ladleful of the soup in a blender or food processor until smooth. Stir the tofu mixture into the soup and simmer for 5 minutes, or until heated through. Serve hot, garnished with the cilantro and scallions.

Chicken & Chipotle Soup

 SERVES 6   PREP TIME: 10 minutes   COOKING TIME: 5 minutes

| nutritional information per serving | 166 cal, 5.5g fat, 1.5g sat fat, 0.3g total sugars, 0.8g salt |

This light but spicy chicken broth is a perfect lunchtime bite for hot summer days.

INGREDIENTS

6 cups chicken stock

2–3 cloves garlic, finely chopped

1–2 dried chipotle chiles, thinly sliced

1 avocado

juice of ½ lime

3–5 scallions, thinly sliced

2½–3 cups bite-size, torn cooked chicken breast

2 tablespoons chopped fresh cilantro

1 lime, cut into wedges, to serve

1. Put the stock in a large saucepan with the garlic and chiles and bring to a boil.

2. Meanwhile, cut the avocado in half around the pit. Twist apart, then remove the pit with a knife. Remove and discard the skin, dice the flesh, and toss in the lime juice to prevent discoloration.

3. Arrange the scallions, chicken, avocado, and cilantro in warm bowls.

4. Ladle hot stock over the bowls' contents and serve immediately with lime wedges.

1

2

2

Mixed Squash Soup

SERVES 4   PREP TIME: 10 minutes   COOKING TIME: 25–30 minutes

nutritional information per serving	169 cal, 7g fat, 2.5g sat fat, 14.5g total sugars, 0.7g salt

Squash makes superb soups with a velvety texture and vivid colors. Mixing the different types gives more interest and flavor, so try buying a selection of what is in season.

INGREDIENTS

1 tablespoon vegetable oil

1 large onion, chopped

1 celery stalk, chopped

2 carrots, chopped

2 cloves garlic, crushed

6 cups peeled, seeded, and cubed mixed winter squash, such as butternut, acorn, delicata, or kabocha squash

4 cups vegetable stock

1 tablespoon fresh thyme leaves, finely chopped

salt and pepper, to taste

crème fraiche or Greek yogurt, to serve

1. Heat the oil in a large saucepan over medium–high heat. Add the onion, celery, and carrots and sweat for 3–4 minutes, or until starting to soften.

2. Add the garlic and squash, and sauté for an additional minute. Add the stock and thyme and season with salt and pepper. Bring to a boil, cover, and simmer for 20 minutes, or until the vegetables are tender.

3. Process using a handheld immersion blender until smooth. Serve immediately, topped with a dollop of crème fraiche or Greek yogurt.

1

2

3

GOES WELL WITH
Serve in the hollowed out crust of a crusty round loaf. Remove the soft inside of the bread with a spoon and set aside to make croutons to serve with the soup.

Spicy Chicken Noodle Soup

 SERVES 2   PREP TIME: 15 minutes   COOKING TIME: 5–10 minutes

nutritional information per serving	513 cal, 10.5g fat, 2.5g sat fat, 8.5g total sugars, 2.1g salt

This quick, healthy, wholesome soup is a real winner for an instant meal that's packed with goodness. The main flavor comes from miso, a highly nutritious fermented paste used as the basis of many noodle soups.

INGREDIENTS

1¼ cups chicken stock

1 tablespoon miso paste

¾-inch piece fresh ginger, peeled and finely grated

1 red chile, seeded and thinly sliced

1 carrot, peeled and cut into thin strips

3 cups coarsely chopped bok choy

6 ounces dried egg cellophane noodles, cooked

1 cooked chicken breast, shredded

dark soy sauce, to taste

4 scallions, trimmed and finely chopped

1. Pour the stock along with 1 cup of boiling water in a saucepan and bring to a boil over medium–high heat. Add the miso paste and simmer for 1–2 minutes.

2. Add the ginger, chile, carrot, bok choy, cooked noodles, and chicken. Simmer for an additional 4–5 minutes. Season with soy sauce.

3. Sprinkle the scallions over the bottom of two serving dishes and pour the soup over them. Serve immediately.

Chunky Vegetable Soup *38*

Broccoli Soup *40*

Chicken Noodle Soup *42*

Mediterranean Vegetable Soup *44*

Carrot & Celery Soup *46*

Beef & Barley Broth *48*

Roast Tomato & Pesto Soup *50*

Zucchini Soup *52*

Carrot & Cilantro Soup *54*

Chicken & Bean Soup *56*

Spiced Winter Squash Soup *58*

Asparagus Soup *60*

Summer Vegetable Soup *62*

Bell Pepper & Tomato Soup *64*

Healthy Soups

Chunky Vegetable Soup

 SERVES 4 | PREP TIME: 10 minutes | COOKING TIME: 15–20 minutes

| nutritional information per serving | 113 cal, 6g fat, 0.7g sat fat, 8g total sugars, 0.4g salt |

This is a hearty, satisfying soup that makes a colorful and nutritious lunch any day of the week. Add seasonal vegetables to make a meal fit for any weather.

INGREDIENTS

1 red onion
1 celery stalk
1 zucchini
2 carrots
2 tablespoons sunflower oil
1 (14½-ounce) can diced tomatoes
3¼ cups vegetable stock
1 large sprig of fresh thyme
salt and pepper, to taste
chopped fresh thyme, to garnish

1. Cut the onion, celery, zucchini, and carrots into ½-inch cubes.

2. Heat the oil in a large saucepan over medium heat. Add the vegetables and sauté, stirring, for 5 minutes without browning.

3. Add the tomatoes, stock, and the thyme sprig. Bring to a boil, then reduce the heat. Cover and simmer for 10–15 minutes, until the vegetables are just tender. Remove and discard the thyme sprig and season with salt and pepper.

4. Transfer the soup to warm serving bowls. Garnish with chopped thyme and serve immediately.

1

2

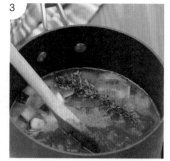
3

Broccoli Soup

nutritional information per serving	104 cal, 0.7g fat, 0.1g sat fat, 1.5g total sugars, 0.5g salt

With few ingredients this soup is quick to whip up and ideal for using any leftover vegetables in the refrigerator.

INGREDIENTS

½ head of broccoli
1 leek, sliced
1 celery stalk, sliced
1 clove garlic, crushed
3 Yukon gold, red-skinnned, or white round potato, diced
4 cups vegetable stock
1 bay leaf
pepper, to taste
toasted croutons, to serve

1. Cut the broccoli into florets and set aside. Cut the thicker broccoli stems into ½-inch dice and put into a large saucepan with the leek, celery, garlic, potato, stock, and bay leaf. Bring to a boil, then reduce the heat, cover, and simmer for 15 minutes.

2. Add the broccoli florets to the soup and return to a boil. Reduce the heat, cover, and simmer for an additional 3–5 minutes, or until the potato and broccoli stems are tender.

3. Remove from the heat and let the soup cool slightly. Remove and discard the bay leaf. Transfer to a food processor or blender, in batches if necessary, and process until smooth.

4. Return the soup to the saucepan and heat through thoroughly. Season with pepper. Ladle the soup into warm bowls and serve immediately with crusty bread or toasted croutons.

1

2

3

GOES WELL WITH
A spoonful of
crème fraîche
or Greek yogurt
is perfect for
cutting through
the soup with
a slightly
acidic tang.

Chicken Noodle Soup

 SERVES 6   PREP TIME: 5 minutes    COOKING TIME: 30–35 minutes

nutritional information per serving   170 cal, 2g fat, 0.5g sat fat, 4g total sugars, 0.7g salt

For many, this is the ultimate cure for winter ailments—it's packed with nutritious ingredients and quickly warms you up.

INGREDIENTS

2 skinless, boneless chicken breasts

5 cups water or chicken stock

3 carrots, peeled and cut into ¼-inch slices

4 ounces egg noodles

salt and pepper, to taste

fresh tarragon leaves, to garnish

1. Put the chicken breasts in a large saucepan over medium heat, add the water, and bring to a simmer. Cook for 25–30 minutes. Skim any foam from the surface, if necessary. Remove the chicken from the stock and keep warm.

2. Continue to simmer the stock, add the carrots and noodles, and cook for 4–5 minutes.

3. Thinly slice or shred the chicken breasts and put in warm serving bowls.

4. Season the soup with salt and pepper and pour it over the chicken. Serve at once, garnished with the tarragon.

Mediterranean Vegetable Soup

 SERVES 6

 PREP TIME: 15 minutes plus standing

 COOKING TIME: 2–2¼ hours

nutritional information per serving	173 cal, 8g fat, 1.5g sat fat, 8g total sugars, 0.7g salt

A real taste of the Mediterranean, with plenty of flavor and little in the way of fat and calories.

INGREDIENTS

2 eggplants

4 tomatoes

2 red bell peppers

2 onions, unpeeled

2 cloves garlic, unpeeled

¼ cup olive oil

1 fresh oregano sprig

6 cups chicken stock or vegetable stock

salt and pepper, to taste

chopped fresh basil, to garnish

1. Preheat the oven to 350°F. Prick the eggplants several times with a fork and put in a roasting pan. Add the tomatoes, bell peppers, and unpeeled onions and garlic. Sprinkle with 2 tablespoons of the oil. Roast in the preheated oven for 30 minutes, then remove the tomatoes. Roast the eggplants, peppers, onions, and garlic for an additional 30 minutes, until soft and the pepper skins have blackened.

2. Put the cooked roasted vegetables in a bowl, cover with a damp dish towel, and let sit for 3–4 hours or overnight, until cold. When cold, cut the eggplants in half, scoop out the flesh, and put in the bowl. Remove the skin from the tomatoes, cut in half and discard the seeds, and add the flesh to the bowl. Hold the bell peppers over the bowl to collect the juices and peel off the skin. Remove the stem, core, and seeds and add the flesh to the bowl. Peel the onions, cut into quarters, and add to the bowl. Squeeze the garlic cloves out of their skin into the bowl.

3. Heat the remaining oil in a large saucepan. Add the vegetables and their juices and the leaves from the oregano sprig, season with salt and pepper, then cook gently, stirring frequently, for 30 minutes. Add the stock and bring to a boil, then simmer for 30 minutes.

4. Remove the saucepan from the heat and let cool slightly. Transfer to a food processor or blender, in batches if necessary, and process until smooth. Return the soup to the rinsed-out pan and reheat gently; do not boil. Ladle into warm bowls, garnish with basil, and serve immediately.

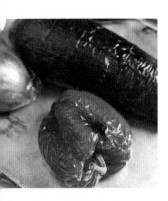

Carrot & Celery Soup

 SERVES 4   PREP TIME: 15 minutes   COOKING TIME: 35–40 minutes

nutritional information
per serving | 174 cal, 3g fat, 1g sat fat, 31g total sugars, 0.5g salt

A wonderful light soup, perfect for days when you want to watch your fat intake without compromising on taste.

INGREDIENTS

15 carrots (about 2 pounds), finely diced
1 onion, chopped
3 celery stalks, diced
4 cups low-sodium vegetable stock
2 Pippin or Gala apples
2 tablespoons tomato paste
1 bay leaf
salt and pepper, to taste

to garnish
1 medium Pippin or Gala apple, thinly sliced
juice of ½ lemon
shredded celery leaves

1. Put the carrots, onion, and celery in a large saucepan and add the stock. Bring to a boil, reduce the heat, cover, and simmer for 10 minutes.

2. Meanwhile, peel, core, and dice the apples. Add the diced apple, tomato paste, and bay leaf to the saucepan and bring to a boil over medium heat. Reduce the heat, cover, and simmer for 20 minutes. Remove and discard the bay leaf.

3. Meanwhile, to make the garnish, put the apple slices in a small saucepan and pour the lemon juice over the slices. Heat the apple slices gently and simmer for 1–2 minutes, or until the apple is tender. Drain the apple slices and reserve until required.

4. Transfer the carrot-and-apple mixture to a food processor or blender, in batches if necessary, and process until smooth. Return the soup to the rinsed-out saucepan, reheat gently, and season with salt and pepper. Ladle the soup into warm bowls, top with the reserved apple slices and shredded celery leaves, and serve immediately.

Beef & Barley Broth

 SERVES 8

 PREP TIME:
15 minutes

 COOKING TIME:
2–2¼ hours

nutritional information
per serving   250 cal, 5.5g fat, 2g sat fat, 5g total sugars, 0.2g salt

Traditionally, in an Irish-style broth, the meat is cut up and divided among individual soup bowls before the broth is poured over. A floury potato for mopping up juices tops each bowl.

INGREDIENTS

1½-pound chuck shoulder beef
⅓ cup pearl barley, rinsed
⅓ cup green split peas, rinsed
1 large onion, thickly sliced
½ teaspoon black peppercorns
3 carrots, halved lengthwise
and sliced
1 small turnip, diced
1 small leek, green parts
included, thinly sliced
1 celery stalk, sliced
8 Yukon gold or
white round potatoes
1 cup shredded green cabbage
salt, to taste
2 tablespoons chopped
fresh parsley

1. Put the beef, pearl barley, and split peas in a large saucepan with the onion and peppercorns. Pour in enough cold water to just cover. Slowly bring to a boil, skim off any foam from the surface, if necessary, then reduce the heat, cover, and simmer gently for 1½ hours.

2. Add the carrots, turnip, leek, and celery to the pan. Season with salt and simmer for an additional 30 minutes. Add a little more water if the soup starts to look too thick.

3. Meanwhile, put the potatoes in another saucepan with water to cover. Add salt to taste and bring to a boil. Cook for 7–10 minutes, until tender but not disintegrating. Drain, return to the pan, and cover with a clean dish cloth.

4. Remove the meat saucepan from the stove. Carefully lift out the meat, using a slotted spoon. Cut into small cubes and return to the pan. Add the cabbage and simmer for an additional 5 minutes, or until the cabbage is just tender. Season with salt, if needed.

5. Ladle the soup into warm wide soup bowls. Put a potato in the middle of each bowl and sprinkle with the parsley.

Roast Tomato & Pesto Soup

 SERVES 4

 PREP TIME:
10 minutes

 COOKING TIME:
25–30 minutes

nutritional information per serving	184 cal, 10.4g fat, 0.6g sat fat, 9g total sugars, 0.6g salt

This soup provides a real taste of summer, and it is a great way to use up a bumper crop of tomatoes from the garden. It's also a light, healthy option, packed with antioxidants, vitamins, and minerals.

INGREDIENTS

1 tablespoon extra virgin olive oil
2 red onions, cut into small wedges
2 cloves garlic, crushed
6 ripe tomatoes
2 cups vegetable stock
salt and pepper, to taste
pesto, to garnish

1. Preheat the oven to 400°F.

2. Put the oil, onions, garlic, and tomatoes in a small roasting pan and toss well to coat. Season generously with salt and pepper.

3. Put in the preheated oven for 25–30 minutes, until the tomatoes are starting to blacken and are softened.

4. Process in a blender or food processor along with the stock, until smooth. Taste and adjust the seasoning, if necessary. Reheat gently.

5. Serve each portion of soup drizzled with a little pesto and a pinch of pepper.

2

3

4

Zucchini Soup

 SERVES 4   PREP TIME: 10 minutes   COOKING TIME: 35–40 minutes

nutritional information per serving	162 cal, 9.5g fat, 5.5g sat fat, 6.5g total sugars, 0.4g salt

Make this soup in the height of summer, when zucchini are most plentiful and cheap to buy. Adjust the strength of the curry flavor to your own personal taste.

INGREDIENTS

½ tablespoon butter

1 large onion, coarsely chopped

4–5 zucchini (about 2 pounds), sliced

2 cups vegetable stock

1 teaspoon curry powder

½ cup sour cream, plus extra to serve

salt and pepper

1. Melt the butter in a large saucepan over medium heat. Add the onion and cook for about 3 minutes, until beginning to soften.

2. Add the zucchini, stock, and curry powder, then season with salt. Bring the soup to a boil, then reduce the heat, cover, and cook gently for about 25 minutes, or until the vegetables are tender.

3. Remove the saucepan from the heat and let cool slightly. Transfer to a food processor or blender, in batches if necessary, and process until smooth.

4. Return the soup to the rinsed-out pan, stir in the sour cream, and reheat gently; do not boil.

5. Taste and adjust the seasoning, adding salt and pepper, if needed. Ladle into warm bowls, top each with a spoonful of sour cream, and serve immediately.

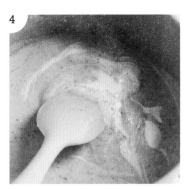

Carrot & Cilantro Soup

 SERVES 6　　 PREP TIME: 15 minutes　　 COOKING TIME: 35–40 minutes

nutritional information per serving	205 cal, 10g fat, 3g sat fat, 9g total sugars, 0.6g salt

This version of the classic soup is made extra special and is packed with flavor by the addition of toasted coriander seeds and plenty of fresh cilantro.

INGREDIENTS

3 tablespoons olive oil

1 red onion, chopped

1 large potato, chopped

1 celery stalk, chopped

8 carrots, chopped

4 cups vegetable stock

1 tablespoon butter

2 teaspoons coriander seeds, crushed

1½ tablespoons chopped fresh cilantro, plus extra to garnish

1 cup milk

salt and pepper, to taste

1. Heat the oil in a large saucepan. Add the onion and cook over low heat, stirring occasionally, for 5 minutes, until softened.

2. Add the potato and celery and cook, stirring occasionally, for 5 minutes, then add the carrots and cook for an additional 5 minutes. Cover the pan, reduce the heat to low, and cook, shaking the pan occasionally, for 10 minutes.

3. Pour in the stock and bring to a boil, then cover and simmer for 10 minutes, until the vegetables are tender.

4. Meanwhile, melt the butter in a skillet. Add the coriander seeds and cook, stirring continuously, for 1 minute. Add the chopped cilantro and cook, stirring continuously, for 1 minute, then remove from the heat.

5. Remove the soup from the heat and let cool slightly. Transfer to a food processor or blender, in batches if necessary, and process until smooth. Return the soup to the rinsed-out pan, stir in the coriander mixture and milk and season with salt and pepper. Reheat gently, then serve, sprinkled with chopped cilantro.

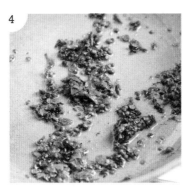

Chicken & Bean Soup

 SERVES 4   *PREP TIME:*
5 minutes   *COOKING TIME:*
20–25 minutes

nutritional information per serving	230 cal, 5.5g fat, 1g sat fat, 12g total sugars, 1.3g salt

A hearty, yet simple dinner with virtually no preparation, the smoky chipotle heat sits well with the tomatoes and beans to make a rich thick meal in a bowl.

INGREDIENTS

1 tablespoon vegetable oil
1 small onion, finely chopped
2 cloves garlic, crushed
1 teaspoon whole cumin seeds
1 tablespoon chipotle paste, or to taste
1 tablespoon tomato paste
½ cup drained and sliced roasted red peppers
1 (14½-ounce) can diced tomatoes
1 cup drained, canned corn kernels
1 (15-ounce) can kidney beans, rinsed and drained
1 cup cooked chicken strips
fresh flat-leaf parsley, finely chopped, to serve
salt and pepper, to taste

1. Heat the oil in a saucepan over medium heat and sauté the onion for 3–4 minutes, until starting to soften.

2. Add the garlic and cumin seeds and cook for an additional minute, then add the chipotle and tomato paste and cook for 1 minute, stirring all the time.

3. Add the roasted red pepper and tomatoes, and season with salt and pepper. Cover and simmer for 10–15 minutes.

4. Stir in the corn, kidney beans, and chicken and reduce the heat to medium–low. Cook for an additional 4–5 minutes. Sprinkle with parsley to serve.

Spiced Winter Squash Soup

 SERVES 4   PREP TIME: 20 minutes   COOKING TIME: 35–40 minutes

| nutritional information per serving | 125 cal, 6g fat, 1g sat fat, 5.5g total sugars, 0.4g salt |

The perfect use for your Halloween pumpkin—scoop out the flesh and carve the tough outer left behind.

INGREDIENTS

2 tablespoons olive oil
1 onion, chopped
1 clove garlic, chopped
1 tablespoon chopped fresh ginger
1 small red chile, seeded and finely chopped
2 tablespoons chopped fresh cilantro, plus extra to garnish
1 bay leaf
8 cups peeled, seeded, and diced pumpkin or other winter squash, or 1 butternut squash, peeled, seeded, and diced
2½ cups vegetable stock
salt and pepper, to taste
light cream, to garnish

1. Heat the oil in a large saucepan over medium heat. Add the onion and garlic and cook for about 4 minutes, until slightly softened. Add the ginger, chile, cilantro, bay leaf, and squash and cook for an additional 3 minutes.

2. Pour in the stock and bring to a boil. Skim any foam from the surface, if necessary. Reduce the heat and simmer, stirring occasionally, for about 25 minutes, or until the pumpkin is tender. Remove from the heat, remove and discard the bay leaf, and let cool.

3. Transfer to a food processor or blender, in batches if necessary, and process until smooth. Return the mixture to the rinsed-out pan and season with salt and pepper.

4. Reheat gently, then remove from the heat and pour into warm soup bowls. Garnish each bowl with a swirl of cream and the cilantro, then serve.

1

2

3

COOK'S NOTE
Don't discard the pumpkin seeds—simply rinse and dry, then put onto a lined baking sheet and toss with oil and salt. Cook in a preheated oven at 275°F for 15 minutes, until golden brown.

Asparagus Soup

 SERVES 6 PREP TIME: 10 minutes  COOKING TIME: 50–55 minutes

nutritional information per serving	240 cal, 16g fat, 10g sat fat, 5.5g total sugars, 0.6g salt

Best made at the height of the asparagus season, this fresh summer soup is completely delicious.

INGREDIENTS

1 bunch asparagus
(about 12 ounces)
3 cups vegetable stock
4 tablespoons butter
1 onion, chopped
3 tablespoons all-purpose flour
¼ teaspoon ground coriander
1 tablespoon lemon juice
2 cups milk
4–6 tablespoons heavy cream
or light cream
salt and pepper, to taste

1. Wash and trim the asparagus, discarding the woody part of the stem. Cut the remainder into short pieces, reserving the tips for garnish.

2. Cook the asparagus tips in ½ inch of boiling water for 5–10 minutes, or until tender. Drain and set aside.

3. Put the asparagus stems in a saucepan with the stock, then bring to a boil, cover, and simmer for about 20 minutes, or until the asparagus is soft. Drain and reserve the stock.

4. Melt the butter in a saucepan. Add the onion and cook over low heat for 3–4 minutes, or until soft. Stir in the flour and cook for 1 minute, then gradually whisk in the reserved stock and bring to a boil.

5. Simmer for 2–3 minutes, until thickened, then stir in the cooked asparagus stems, coriander, and lemon juice and season with salt and pepper. Simmer for 10 minutes. Remove the saucepan from the heat and let cool slightly. Transfer to a food processor or blender, in batches if necessary, and process until smooth.

6. Return the soup to the rinsed-out pan, add the milk and reserved asparagus tips, and bring to a boil. Simmer for 2 minutes. Stir in the cream and reheat gently; do not boil. Ladle into warm bowls and serve immediately.

Summer Vegetable Soup

SERVES 4   PREP TIME: 20 minutes   COOKING TIME: 20–25 minutes

nutritional information per serving	207 cal, 4g fat, 0.7g sat fat, 4.5g total sugars, 0.8g salt

Wonderfully fresh and light, and bursting with the flavors of summer, this soup is delicious to eat and sturdy enough to fill you until dinner.

INGREDIENTS

1 tablespoon vegetable oil

1 onion, finely chopped

2 cloves garlic, crushed

1 whole fennel bulb, trimmed and diced

1 leek, finely sliced

1 large potato, diced

4 cups vegetable stock

3½ cups spinach, trimmed

6 asparagus spears, trimmed and cut into short lengths

1⅓ cups frozen peas

handful fresh basil leaves, thinly sliced

salt and pepper, to taste

1. Heat the oil in a saucepan over medium heat and sauté the onion for 5 minutes. Add the garlic, fennel, leek, and potato and cook for an additional 1–2 minutes.

2. Add the stock and season with salt and pepper. Cover and simmer for 15 minutes.

3. Add the spinach, asparagus, and peas and cook for an additional 2–3 minutes.

4. Stir in the basil leaves, adjust the seasoning, if necessary, and serve.

1

2

3

SOMETHING DIFFERENT

Try varying the vegetables according to the season. Keep the base the same, using onion, garlic, fennel, potato, and leek, but use other vegetables such as kale or fava beans.

Bell Pepper & Tomato Soup

 SERVES 4   PREP TIME: 5 minutes   COOKING TIME: 20–25 minutes

nutritional information per serving	125 cal, 4g fat, 0.5g sat fat, 13.5g total sugars, 0.5g salt

This vibrant soup is packed with health-boosting antioxidants, plus it's incredibly quick to make because it uses store-bought roasted red peppers; a great pantry standby for speedy dinners.

INGREDIENTS

1 tablespoon vegetable oil
1 onion, chopped
2 cloves garlic, chopped
1½ teaspoons hot chili powder
2 tablespoons tomato paste
2¼ cups drained and chopped roasted red peppers
1 (28-ounce) can diced tomatoes
1¾ cups vegetable stock
salt and pepper, to taste

1. Heat the oil in a saucepan over medium heat. Add the onion and garlic and sauté for 3–4 minutes, until starting to soften.

2. Add the chili powder and tomato paste and cook for 1 minute, stirring continuously.

3. Add the roasted red peppers, tomatoes, and stock and season with salt and pepper. Stir well, cover, and simmer for 15 minutes.

4. Process in a blender or food processor, until smooth. Adjust the seasoning, if necessary, and serve.

2

3

3

GOES WELL WITH
Delicious served with goat cheese crumbled over the top, and a generous drizzle of olive oil.

Lentil & Spinach Soup *68*

Jerusalem Artichoke Soup *70*

Split Pea & Ham Soup *72*

Minestrone Soup *74*

Tomato & White Bean Soup *76*

Meatball Soup *78*

New England Clam Chowder *80*

Rustic Bread, Basil & Tomato Soup *82*

Potato & Pesto Soup *84*

Spiced Chickpea & Spinach Soup *86*

Chilli Chicken Soup *88*

Cream of Mushroom Soup *90*

Turkey, Sage, & Mushroom Soup *92*

Roast Sweet Potato & Garlic Soup *94*

Hearty Soups

Delicious

Lentil & Spinach Soup

 SERVES 4 PREP TIME: 10 minutes 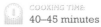 COOKING TIME: 40–45 minutes

nutritional information • per serving	270 cal, 2.5g fat, 0.5g sat fat, 8g total sugars, 0.9g salt

A wonderful fresh and fragrant soup—light yet packed with flavor and nutrients, this soup is simple to make and great to eat at any time of the day.

INGREDIENTS

1 teaspoon vegetable oil
1 onion, finely chopped
2 cloves garlic, finely chopped
2 celery stalks, finely chopped
3 carrots, peeled and finely chopped
½ teaspoon chili powder
1 teaspoon smoked paprika
1 teaspoon whole cumin seeds
1 cup dried red lentils, washed
4 cups vegetable stock
1 cup coarsely chopped spinach, thawed if frozen
6 cherry tomatoes, halved
¼ cup plain yogurt, to serve
salt and pepper

1. Heat the oil in a large saucepan over medium heat. Add the onion, garlic, celery, and carrots, and cook for 4–5 minutes, or until starting to soften.

2. Add the chili powder, paprika, and cumin seeds and cook for an additional 1 minute, stirring continuously.

3. Add the lentils and stock, season with salt and pepper, bring to a boil, and cook for 10 minutes. Cover and reduce the heat, then simmer for 20–25 minutes, until the vegetables and lentils are cooked.

4. Add the spinach and tomatoes and cook for 5 minutes, or until the spinach has wilted. Season with salt and pepper, if necessary. Serve immediately with a tablespoon of yogurt in each bowl.

Jerusalem Artichoke Soup

 SERVES 6

 PREP TIME:
10 minutes

 COOKING TIME:
45–50 minutes

nutritional information per serving	306 cal, 21.5g fat, 11.5g sat fat, 4.5g total sugars, 0.8g salt

Jerusalem artichokes lend themselves perfectly to this velvety soup because they break down quickly and easily. Their sweet nutty flavor is delicious with the tangy chives, making a wonderfully comforting winter treat.

INGREDIENTS

1 tablespoon lemon juice
1½ pounds Jerusalem artichokes
4 tablespoons butter
1 tablespoon sunflower oil
1 onion, chopped
5½ cups vegetable stock
¾ cup milk
1 tablespoon snipped fresh chives, plus extra to garnish
½ cup heavy cream
salt and pepper, to taste
extra virgin olive oil, for drizzling
croutons, to serve

1. Fill a bowl with water and stir in the lemon juice. Peel the artichokes and cut into chunks, then immediately drop them into the water to prevent discoloration.

2. Heat the butter with the sunflower oil in a large saucepan. Add the onion and cook over low heat, stirring occasionally, for 5 minutes, until softened. Drain the artichokes, add them to the pan, and stir well. Cover and cook, stirring occasionally, for 15 minutes.

3. Pour in the stock and milk, increase the heat to medium, and bring to a boil. Reduce the heat, replace the lid, and simmer for 20 minutes, until the artichokes are soft.

4. Remove the pan from the heat and let cool slightly. Add the chives and transfer the soup to a food processor or blender, in batches if necessary, and process until smooth.

5. Return the soup to the rinsed-out pan, stir in the cream, and season with salt and pepper. Reheat gently, then ladle into warm bowls, drizzle with extra virgin olive oil, and serve immediately with croutons and chives

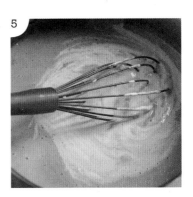

Split Pea & Ham Soup

SERVES 8   PREP TIME: 10 minutes   COOKING TIME: 1½–1¾ hours

nutritional information per serving   280 cal, 15g fat, 6g sat fat, 4.5g total sugars, 2.4g salt

This thick and tasty soup is sometimes called "London Particular" after the so-called "peasouper" fogs that engulfed London in the nineteenth century.

INGREDIENTS

2½ cups split green peas
1 tablespoon olive oil
1 large onion, finely chopped
1 large carrot, finely chopped
1 celery stalk, finely chopped
4 cups chicken stock
or vegetable stock
4 cups water
8 ounces lean smoked ham,
finely diced
¼ teaspoon dried thyme
¼ teaspoon dried marjoram
1 bay leaf
salt and pepper, to taste

1. Rinse the peas under cold running water. Put them in a saucepan and cover with water. Bring to the boil and boil for 3 minutes, skimming any foam from the surface, if necessary. Drain the peas.

2. Heat the oil in a large saucepan over a medium heat. Add the onion and cook for 3–4 minutes, stirring occasionally, until just softened. Add the carrot and celery and continue cooking for 2 minutes.

3. Add the peas, pour over the stock and water and stir to combine.

4. Bring just to the boil and stir the ham into the soup. Add the thyme, marjoram and bay leaf. Reduce the heat, cover and cook gently for 1–1½ hours, until the ingredients are very soft. Remove the bay leaf.

5. Taste and adjust the seasoning. Ladle into warmed soup bowls and serve.

1

2

3

Minestrone Soup

 SERVES 4   PREP TIME: 20 minutes    COOKING TIME: 45–50 minutes

nutritional information per serving	352 cal, 9.5g fat, 2g sat fat, 12.5g total sugars, 1.8g salt

To Italians, "minestrone" means "big soup." It's a great way to use up leftover vegetables and make a wholesome meal big enough to feed a family.

INGREDIENTS

2 tablespoons olive oil

2 cloves garlic, chopped

2 red onions, chopped

3 ounces prosciutto, sliced

1 red bell pepper, seeded and chopped

1 orange bell pepper, seeded and chopped

1 (14½-ounce) can diced tomatoes

4 cups vegetable stock

1 celery stalk, chopped

1 (15-ounce) can cranberry beans, drained

1 cup shredded green cabbage

½ cup frozen peas

1 tablespoon chopped fresh parsley

3 ounces dried vermicelli pasta

salt and pepper, to taste

freshly grated Parmesan cheese, to serve

1. Heat the oil in a large saucepan. Add the garlic, onions, and prosciutto and cook over medium heat, stirring, for 3 minutes, until slightly softened.

2. Add the red bell pepper and orange bell pepper and the diced tomatoes and cook for an additional 2 minutes, stirring. Stir in the stock, then add the celery.

3. Add the beans to the pan with the cabbage, peas, and parsley. Season with salt and pepper. Bring to a boil, then reduce the heat and simmer for 30 minutes.

4. Add the pasta to the pan and cook according to the package directions, until tender but still firm to the bite. Remove from the heat and ladle into bowls. Sprinkle with Parmesan cheese and serve.

Tomato & White Bean Soup

 SERVES 6

 PREP TIME:
30 minutes

 COOKING TIME:
30–35 minutes

nutritional information
per serving | 240 cal, 9g fat, 2.5g sat fat, 12g total sugars, 0.7g salt

This recipe is perfect for using up a bumper crop of tomatoes in the late summer and is also low in fat.

INGREDIENTS

3 tablespoons olive oil

2 red onions, finely chopped

1 celery stalk, finely chopped

1 red bell pepper, seeded and finely chopped

2 cloves garlic, finely chopped

16 plum tomatoes, peeled and chopped

5½ cups vegetable stock

2 tablespoons tomato paste

1 teaspoon sugar

1 tablespoon sweet paprika

1 tablespoon butter

1 tablespoon all-purpose flour

1 (15-ounce) can cannellini beans, rinsed and drained

salt and pepper, to taste

chopped fresh flat-leaf parsley, to garnish

1. Heat the olive oil in a large saucepan. Add the onions, celery, red bell pepper, and garlic and cook over low heat, stirring occasionally, for 5 minutes, until softened.

2. Increase the heat to medium, add the tomatoes, and cook, stirring occasionally, for an additional 5 minutes, then pour in the stock. Stir in the tomato paste, sugar, and sweet paprika and season with salt and pepper. Bring to a boil, reduce the heat, and simmer for 15 minutes.

3. Meanwhile, mash together the butter and flour to a paste in a small bowl with a fork. Stir the paste, small pieces at a time, into the soup. Make sure each piece is fully incorporated before adding the next.

4. Add the beans, stir well, and simmer for an additional 5 minutes, until heated through. Sprinkle with the parsley and serve immediately.

Meatball Soup

nutritional information per serving	260 cal, 9g fat, 4g sat fat, 1g total sugars, 1.5g salt

A delicious broth with meatballs and mini pasta, this is made into a complete meal with the addition of the greens.

INGREDIENTS

12 ounces ground round or ground sirloin beef

¼ cup finely grated onion

2 tablespoons freshly grated Parmesan cheese, plus extra to serve

½ teaspoon pepper, or to taste

¼ teaspoon salt, or to taste

1 medium egg, beaten

8½ cups chicken stock,

2 ounces dried soup pasta

3¾ cups trimmed and finely shredded Swiss chard or savoy cabbage

1. Preheat the oven to 450°F.

2. Combine the beef, onion, Parmesan, ½ teaspoon of pepper, and ¼ teaspoon of salt in a bowl, mixing well with a fork. Stir in the beaten egg. Shape into 24 walnut-size balls and place on a nonstick baking sheet. Cook in the preheated oven for 5–7 minutes, turning once, until lightly browned. Remove from the oven and set aside.

3. Bring the stock to a boil in a large saucepan. Add the pasta and meatballs, then let simmer for 10 minutes.

4. Meanwhile, steam the Swiss chard for 2–3 minutes, until wilted. Transfer to a strainer and squeeze out as much liquid as possible, pressing with the back of a wooden spoon. Add the Swiss chard to the soup and cook for 5 minutes, or until the greens and pasta are tender.

5. Taste and season with salt and pepper, if needed. Ladle the soup into warm bowls and serve immediately with Parmesan.

2

3

4

FREEZING TIP

The meatballs can be frozen— simply follow the recipe until you've made the 24 walnut-size balls, then put in an airtight container, layer with parchment paper, seal, and freeze for up to three months.

New England Clam Chowder

 SERVES 4   PREP TIME: 15 minutes   COOKING TIME: 25 minutes

nutritional information per serving	890 cal, 73g fat, 42g sat fat, 6.5g total sugars, 2.7g salt

*Delicious classic New-England-style chowder,
rich and creamy with a salty hit of bacon and
thickened with potatoes.*

INGREDIENTS

2 pounds fresh clams, scrubbed

4 bacon strips, chopped

2 tablespoons butter, plus extra for frying

1 onion, chopped

1 tablespoon chopped fresh thyme

1 Yukon gold or white round large potato, diced

1¼ cups milk

1 bay leaf

1½ cups heavy cream

1 tablespoon chopped fresh parsley

salt and pepper, to taste

1. Put the clams in a large saucepan with a splash of water. Cook over high heat for 3–4 minutes, until they open. Discard any that remain closed. Strain, reserving the cooking liquid. Let sit until cool enough to handle, reserving eight for the garnish.

2. Remove the clams from their shells, chopping them coarsely if large, and reserve.

3. In a clean saucepan, cook the bacon with a little butter until browned and crisp. Drain on paper towels. Add the butter to the same saucepan, and when it has melted, add the onion. Sauté for 4–5 minutes, until soft but not browned. Add the thyme and cook briefly before adding the diced potato, reserved clam cooking liquid, milk, and bay leaf. Bring to a boil, then reduce the heat and let simmer for 10 minutes, or until the potato is just tender.

4. Discard the bay leaf, then transfer to a food processor and process until smooth, or push through a strainer into a bowl.

5. Add the clams, bacon, and cream. Simmer for an additional 2–3 minutes, until heated through. Season with salt and pepper. Stir in the chopped parsley and serve, garnished with the reserved clams in their shells.

Rustic Bread, Basil & Tomato Soup

SERVES 4

PREP TIME:
10 minutes

COOKING TIME:
25–30 minutes

nutritional information per serving	226 cal, 6g fat, 2g sat fat, 5.5g total sugars, 1.3g salt

Not only a great way of using up leftover bread, this soup is also a simple dinner to whip up if you're in a hurry—with very little prep needed.

INGREDIENTS

1 tablespoon olive oil

1 onion, finely chopped

2 cloves garlic, crushed

1 (14½-ounce) can whole plum tomatoes

2½ cups chicken stock or vegetable stock

7 slices day-old, unsliced white bread, cubed

handful fresh basil, coarsely chopped, plus extra to garnish

salt and pepper, to taste

Parmesan cheese, to serve

1. Heat the oil in a saucepan over medium heat. Add the onion and garlic and sauté for 4–5 minutes.

2. Add the tomatoes and stock, and use the back of a wooden spoon to break the tomatoes apart. Season with salt and pepper, cover, and simmer for 15 minutes.

3. Add the bread and basil and simmer for an additional 5 minutes.

4. Serve with Parmesan cheese shavings sprinkled over the top, garnished with the chopped basil and seasoned with pepper.

1

2

3

SOMETHING
DIFFERENT
If you have a
bumper crop of
fresh tomatoes to
use up, toss four
of them in a little
oil, then roast in
a hot oven for
about 20 minutes.
Add to the soup
in place of the
canned tomatoes.

Potato & Pesto Soup

 SERVES 4

 PREP TIME:
20 minutes

 COOKING TIME:
40–45 minutes

nutritional information per serving	1076 cal, 83g fat, 29g sat fat, 15g total sugars, 1.6g salt

Creamy potatoes and pasta contrast wonderfully with homemade pesto to make a fresh-tasting, filling soup.

INGREDIENTS

2 tablespoons olive oil

3 rindless bacon strips, finely chopped

2 tablespoons butter

4 Yukon gold, red-skinned, or white round potatoes, chopped

3 onions, finely chopped

2½ cups chicken stock

2½ cups milk

4 ounces dried conchigliette (small pasta shells)

⅔ cup heavy cream

2 tablespoons chopped fresh parsley

salt and pepper, to taste

pesto

1 cup finely chopped fresh parsley

2 cloves garlic, crushed

⅓ cup pine nuts, crushed

2 tablespoons chopped fresh basil leaves

⅔ cup freshly grated Parmesan cheese, plus extra to serve

⅔ cup olive oil

white pepper, to taste

1. To make the pesto, put all of the ingredients in a food processor or blender and process for 2 minutes to form a coarse paste. Scrape into a small bowl and set aside.

2. Heat the oil in a large saucepan and cook the bacon over medium heat for 4 minutes. Add the butter, potatoes, and onions and cook, stirring continuously, for 12 minutes.

3. Add the stock and milk to the saucepan, bring to a boil, and simmer for 10 minutes. Add the pasta and simmer for an additional 3–4 minutes.

4. Stir in the cream and simmer for 5 minutes. Add the parsley, season with salt and pepper, and stir in 2 tablespoons of the pesto. Ladle the soup into warm bowls, sprinkle with Parmesan cheese, and serve immediately.

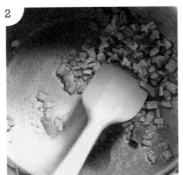

Spiced Chickpea
& Spinach Soup

 SERVES 4 PREP TIME:
5 minutes 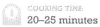 COOKING TIME:
20–25 minutes

nutritional information per serving	181 cal, 6.5g fat, 1g sat fat, 6.5g total sugars, 1g salt

Enjoy a warming blend of aromatic herbs and spices. The addition of the mint dressing makes a delicious, cooling topping that complements the subtle heat of the soup.

INGREDIENTS

1 tablespoon vegetable oil
1 onion, finely chopped
2 cloves garlic, crushed
1 teaspoon whole cumin seeds
2 teaspoons medium curry powder
1 teaspoon hot chili powder
1 (15-ounce) can chickpeas, rinsed and drained
1 (14½-ounce) can diced tomatoes
2 cups vegetable stock
3½ cups chopped spinach, thawed if frozen
salt and pepper, to taste

mint dressing
½ cup plain yogurt
2 tablespoons fresh mint leaves, finely chopped

1. Heat the oil in a saucepan over medium heat. Add the onion and sauté for 4–5 minutes, or until starting to soften.

2. Add the garlic, cumin seeds, curry powder, and chili powder and cook for 1 minute, stirring continuously.

3. Add the chickpeas, tomatoes, and stock and season with salt and pepper. Bring to a boil, then reduce the heat, cover, and simmer for 15 minutes.

4. Meanwhile, to make the mint dressing, add the yogurt and mint to a bowl, season with salt and pepper, and mix together. Cover and chill until ready to serve.

5. Stir the spinach into the soup and cook for an additional 1–2 minutes, or until the spinach has wilted. Serve with a little of the mint dressing drizzled over the soup.

Chilli Chicken Soup

 SERVES 4   PREP TIME: 15 minutes    COOKING TIME: 25–30 minutes

nutritional information per serving	251 cal, 8g fat, 1.5g sat fat, 12g total sugars, 0.8g salt

This deliciously fresh and zingy soup produces an explosion of flavors on the palate. It has a light chile kick, which you can adjust to suit your taste.

INGREDIENTS

1 tablespoon vegetable oil

1 onion, finely chopped

2 celery stalks, finely chopped

2 carrots, finely chopped

1 red chile, seeded and finely chopped

2 cloves garlic, crushed

2 tablespoons tomato paste

1 tablespoon fresh oregano, finely chopped

2½ cups drained, canned whole tomatoes

2 cups chicken stock

2 skinless, boneless chicken breasts, cubed

juice of 1 lime

salt and pepper, to taste

to garnish

½ bunch scallions, finely chopped

½ avocado, peeled, pitted, and finely chopped

4 teaspoons chopped fresh cilantro

tortilla chips, crumbled

1. Heat the oil in a large saucepan and sauté the onion, celery, carrots, chile, and garlic and cook for 4–5 minutes.

2. Add the tomato paste and cook for an additional 1 minute, stirring continuously.

3. Add the oregano, tomatoes, and stock and bring to a gentle simmer, breaking down the tomatoes with the back of a wooden spoon to release the juices.

4. Add the chicken, season with salt and pepper, cover, and cook for an additional 20 minutes.

5. Remove from the heat, stir in the lime juice, and ladle the soup into serving bowls. Serve each portion topped with a selection of garnishes.

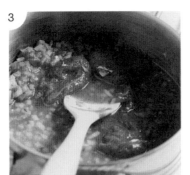

Cream of Mushroom Soup

 SERVES 4

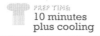 PREP TIME:
10 minutes
plus cooling

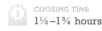 COOKING TIME:
1½–1¾ hours

nutritional information per serving	600 cal, 55g fat, 34.5g sat fat, 3g total sugars, 0.7g salt

The secret to this delicious soup is patience. The longer you cook and caramelize the mushrooms in the butter, the deeper and "meatier" the flavor will be. Take your time and you'll be richly rewarded.

INGREDIENTS

1 stick unsalted butter

13 cups thickly sliced white button mushrooms (about 2 pounds)

1 onion, coarsely chopped

1 tablespoon flour

4 cups chicken stock

1 cup water

6 sprigs fresh thyme, plus picked leaves to garnish

3 cloves garlic

1 cup heavy cream

salt and pepper, to taste

1. Melt the butter in a large saucepan over medium heat. Add the mushrooms and a pinch of salt. Cook, stirring occasionally, for 20–30 minutes, or until the mushrooms are golden brown. Reserve some of the browned mushrooms to garnish the soup later on.

2. Add the onions and cook over medium–low heat for about 5 minutes. Add the flour and cook, stirring, for 1 minute. Whisk in the stock and water. Add the thyme and garlic and bring to a simmer. Reduce the heat to low, cover, and simmer gently for 1 hour.

3. Remove the soup from the heat, uncover, and let cool for 15 minutes. Transfer to a food processor or blender, in batches if necessary, and process until smooth.

4. Return the soup to the rinsed-out pan and gently reheat; do not boil. Add the cream and adjust the seasoning, if necessary. Serve hot, topped with the reserved mushrooms and thyme leaves.

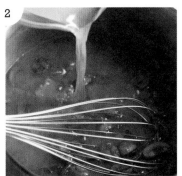

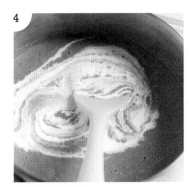

Turkey, Sage, & Mushroom Soup

 SERVES 6   PREP TIME: 20 minutes   COOKING TIME: 1–1¼ hours

nutritional information per serving	421 cal, 15g fat, 5.3g sat fat, 2g total sugars, 0.7g salt

Bridging the gap between risotto and stroganoff, this soup is a really filling staple for dinner.

INGREDIENTS

3 tablespoons butter

1 onion, finely chopped

1 celery stalk, finely chopped

25 large fresh sage leaves, finely chopped

4 tablespoons all-purpose flour

5 cups chicken stock

½ cup brown rice

3½ cups sliced white button mushrooms

1½ cups diced, cooked turkey,

1 cup heavy cream

salt and pepper, to taste

sprigs of fresh sage, to garnish

freshly grated Parmesan cheese, to serve

1. Melt half the butter in a large saucepan over medium–low heat. Add the onion, celery, and sage and cook for 3–4 minutes, until the onion is softened, stirring frequently. Stir in the flour and continue cooking for 2 minutes.

2. Slowly add about one-quarter of the stock and stir well, scraping the bottom of the pan to mix in the flour. Pour in the remaining stock, stirring to combine completely, and bring just to a boil.

3. Stir in the rice and season with salt and pepper. Reduce the heat and simmer gently, partly covered, for about 30 minutes, until the rice is just tender, stirring occasionally.

4. Meanwhile, melt the remaining butter in a large skillet over medium heat. Add the mushrooms and season with salt and pepper. Cook for about 8 minutes, until they are golden brown, stirring occasionally at first, then more often after they start to brown. Add the mushrooms to the soup.

5. Add the turkey to the soup and stir in the cream. Continue simmering for about 10 minutes, until heated through. Taste and adjust the seasoning, if necessary. Ladle into serving bowls, garnish with sage, and serve with Parmesan cheese.

Roast Sweet Potato & Garlic Soup

 SERVES 6 PREP TIME: 5 minutes 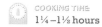 COOKING TIME: 1¼ –1½ hours

nutritional information per serving	226 cal, 11g fat, 5g sat fat, 9g total sugars, 0.5g salt

This soup has an appetizing combination of color and taste—roasting the root vegetables intensifies their sweet, earthy flavors.

INGREDIENTS

1 acorn or butternut squash
2 large sweet potatoes
4 shallots
2 tablespoons olive oil
6 cloves garlic, unpeeled
3½ cups chicken stock
½ cup crème fraîche
or Greek yogurt
salt and pepper, to taste
snipped fresh chives, to garnish

1. Preheat the oven to 375°F. Cut the squash, sweet potato, and shallots in half lengthwise, all the way to the stem end. Scoop the seeds out of the squash. Brush a shallow roasting pan with the oil.

2. Put the vegetables, cut side down, in the prepared pan and add the garlic. Roast in the preheated oven for about 40 minutes, until tender and light brown. Set aside and let cool.

3. When cool, scoop the flesh from the sweet potato and squash halves and put in a saucepan. Peel the shallots and garlic and add to the other vegetables.

4. Add the stock. Bring just to a boil, reduce the heat, and simmer, partly covered, for about 30 minutes, stirring occasionally, until the vegetables are tender.

5. Let the soup cool slightly, then transfer to a food processor and process, in batches if necessary, until smooth.

6. Return the soup to the rinsed-out saucepan. Season with salt and pepper, then simmer for 5–10 minutes, until heated through. Stir in the crème fraîche or yogurt, then ladle into serving bowls, garnish with snipped chives, and serve.

Southwest Vegetable Soup *98*

Wonton Soup *100*

Lobster Bisque *102*

Avocado Soup with Guacamole Toasts *104*

Chicken & Mushroom Soup with Puff Pastry *106*

Clam & Pasta Soup *108*

Roasted Pumpkin, Garlic & Thyme Soup *110*

Borscht *112*

Miso Soup *114*

Crab & Ginger Soup *116*

Salmon Ramen Soup *118*

French Onion Soup *120*

Vietnamese Crab Soup *122*

Mixed Bean Soup with Gruyère *124*

Around the World

Southwest Vegetable Soup

 SERVES 6

 PREP TIME: 25 minutes

 COOKING TIME: 35–40 minutes

nutritional information per serving	150 cal, 5g fat, 0.5g sat fat, 6g total sugars, 0.6g salt

More than just a soup, this is a big bowl bursting with the flavors and spices of the Southwest. It's a complete meal in a bowl, an explosion of big flavors and color, and all that in under an hour of cooking!

INGREDIENTS

2 tablespoons vegetable oil

1 onion, finely chopped

4 cloves garlic, finely chopped

¼–½ teaspoon ground cumin

2–3 teaspoons mild chili powder

1 carrot, sliced

1 Yukon gold, red-skinned, or white round potato, diced

3 fresh tomatoes, diced

1 zucchini, diced

¼ small head of cabbage, cored and finely shredded

about 4 cups vegetable stock or chicken stock

1 fresh corn cob or 2 cups corn kernels, thawed if frozen

10 green beans, cut into bite-size lengths

salt and pepper, to taste

chopped fresh cilantro and sliced fresh green chile, to garnish

tortilla chips, to serve

1. Heat the oil in a large saucepan over medium heat. Add the onion and garlic and cook for 3–4 minutes, until softened, then sprinkle in the cumin and chili powder. Stir in the carrot, potato, tomatoes, zucchini, and cabbage and cook, stirring occasionally, for 2 minutes.

2. Pour in the stock. Cover and cook over medium heat for 20 minutes, or until the vegetables are tender.

3. Meanwhile, remove and discard the husks and silks from the corn cob, then cut off the kernels, using a small sharp knife. Add a little extra stock to the soup, if needed, then stir in the corn kernels and beans and cook for an additional 5–10 minutes, or until the beans are tender. Season with salt and pepper.

4. Ladle the soup into warm bowls and garnish with cilantro and chile. Serve immediately with tortilla chips.

Wonton Soup

 SERVES 6 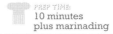 PREP TIME: 10 minutes plus marinading COOKING TIME: 5–10 minutes

| nutritional information per serving | 122 cal, 3g fat, 1g sat fat, 2g total sugars, 1.4g salt |

The little Chinese packages are lightly poached in the soup broth to produce a tender finish.

INGREDIENTS

6 ounces ground pork or chicken

2 ounces peeled shrimp, ground

1 scallion, finely chopped

1 teaspoon finely chopped fresh ginger

1 teaspoon sugar

1 tablespoon Chinese rice wine or dry sherry

2 tablespoons light soy sauce

24 store-bought wonton wrappers

8½ cups vegetable stock

snipped fresh chives, to garnish

1. Mix together the pork, shrimp, scallion, ginger, sugar, rice wine, and half the soy sauce in a bowl until thoroughly combined. Cover and let marinate for 20 minutes.

2. Put 1 teaspoon of the mixture in the center of each wonton wrapper. Dampen the edges, fold corner to corner into a triangle, and press to seal, then seal together the two remaining corners.

3. Bring the stock to a boil in a large saucepan. Add the wontons and cook for 5 minutes. Stir in the remaining soy sauce and remove from the heat. Ladle the soup and wontons into warm bowls, sprinkle with snipped chives, and serve immediately.

1

2

3
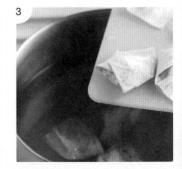

FREEZING TIP

Make the wonton packages in advance by following the first two steps. Then place on a lined baking sheet and put in the freezer. Once frozen, transfer to an airtight container and store for up to three months.

Lobster Bisque

 SERVES 4　　 *PREP TIME:* 30 minutes　　 *COOKING TIME:* 45–50 minutes

nutritional information per serving	454 cal, 24g fat, 14g sat fat, 5g total sugars, 1.1g salt

This elegant, smooth, and delicious soup is perfect for entertaining and bound to impress your guests.

INGREDIENTS

1 pound cooked lobster
3 tablespoons butter
1 small carrot, shredded
1 celery stalk, finely chopped
1 leek, finely chopped
1 small onion, finely chopped
2 shallots, finely chopped
3 tablespoons brandy or Cognac
¼ cup dry white wine
5 cups water
1 tablespoon tomato paste
½ cup heavy cream, or to taste
⅓ cup all-purpose flour
2–3 tablespoons cold water
salt and pepper, to taste
snipped fresh chives, to garnish

1. Pull off the lobster tail. With the legs up, cut the body in half lengthwise. Scoop out the tomalley and the roe. Reserve these, cover, and chill in the refrigerator. Remove the meat from the rest of the lobster and cut into bite-size pieces, then cover and chill in the refrigerator. Chop the shell into large pieces.

2. Melt half the butter in a large saucepan over medium heat and add the lobster shell pieces. Sauté until brown pieces begin to stick to the bottom of the pan. Add the carrot, celery, leek, onion, and shallots. Cook, stirring continuously, for 1–2 minutes. Add the brandy and wine and simmer for 1 minute. Pour in the water, add the tomato paste and a large pinch of salt, and bring to a boil. Reduce the heat and simmer for 30 minutes, then strain the stock, discarding the solids.

3. Melt the remaining butter in a small saucepan and add the tomalley and roe. Add the cream and whisk to mix well, then remove from the heat and set aside. Put the flour in a small mixing bowl and slowly whisk in the cold water. Stir in a little of the hot stock mixture to make a smooth liquid.

4. Bring the remaining lobster stock to a boil and whisk in the flour mixture. Boil gently for 4–5 minutes, or until the soup thickens. Press the tomalley, roe, and cream mixture through a strainer into the soup, then add the lobster meat. Simmer until heated through.

5. Taste and adjust the seasoning, adding salt and pepper, if needed. Stir in a little more cream, if desired. Ladle into warm bowls, garnish with chives, and serve immediately.

Avocado Soup with Guacamole Toasts

 SERVES 6 PREP TIME: 15 minutes COOKING TIME: 30–35 minutes

nutritional information per serving	476 cal, 39g fat, 15g sat fat, 3.5g total sugars, 1g salt

Cooking the avocado brings out its buttery sweetness, which contrasts with the crispy texture of the toasts.

INGREDIENTS

3 ripe avocados
2 tablespoons lemon juice
6 tablespoons butter
6 shallots, chopped
1½ tablespoons all-purpose flour
3½ cups vegetable stock
¾ cup light cream
salt and pepper, to taste
extra virgin olive oil, for drizzling
1 lime, thinly sliced, to garnish

guacamole toasts
6 thin slices of day-old baguette
olive oil, for brushing
½ large ripe avocado, pitted and brushed with lime juice
juice of 1 lime
½ teaspoon hot pepper sauce, or to taste

1. Halve the avocados lengthwise and gently twist the halves apart. Remove and discard the pits and scoop out the flesh. Chop into small pieces, put them into a bowl, sprinkle with the lemon juice, and toss well to coat.

2. Melt the butter in a saucepan. Add the shallots and cook over low heat, stirring occasionally, for 5 minutes, until softened. Stir in the flour and cook, stirring continuously, for 1 minute. Remove the pan from the heat and gradually stir in the stock. Return the pan to medium heat and bring to a boil, stirring continuously.

3. Add the chopped avocado, reduce the heat, cover, and simmer for 15 minutes.

4. Meanwhile, to make the guacamole toasts, preheat the broiler. Toast the bread on one side under the preheated broiler. Turn the slices over, brush with oil, and toast the second side. Remove from the heat. Scoop out the avocado flesh into a bowl, mash with the lime juice and hot pepper sauce, and season with salt and pepper. Divide the avocado mixture among the toasts and set aside.

5. Remove the soup from the heat and push it through a strainer set over a bowl. Return the strained soup to the rinsed-out pan, stir in the cream, and reheat gently; do not boil. Season with salt and pepper.

6. Ladle the soup into warm bowls, drizzle with olive oil, and garnish with the lime slices. Serve with the guacamole toasts.

Chicken & Mushroom Soup with Puff Pastry

 SERVES 4

 PREP TIME
10 minutes

 COOKING TIME
1–1¼ hours

nutritional information
per serving : 716 cal, 37g fat, 18.5g sat fat, 4g total sugars, 1.8g salt

The base of this soup is an mixture of cider and chicken stock that's delicious with the pastry top.

INGREDIENTS

2 chicken legs, skin removed

4 cups chicken stock

⅔ cup apple cider or apple juice

1 onion, finely chopped

1 bay leaf

4 cups thickly sliced cremini mushrooms

¼ cup cornstarch blended with ¼ cup water

¼ cup crème fraîche or heavy cream

salt and pepper, to taste

flour for sprinkling

1 sheet ready-to-bake puff pastry

1. Put the chicken legs in a large saucepan with the stock, cider or juice, onion, and bay leaf. Cover and simmer for 25 minutes. Add the mushrooms and simmer for an additional 10 minutes. Remove the chicken and set aside. Remove and discard the bay leaf.

2. Stir the cornstarch into the stock. Heat, stirring continuously, until boiling and thickened. Remove from the heat and let cool. Remove the meat from the chicken legs and tear into pieces.

3. Preheat the oven to 400°F. Stir the chicken and crème fraîche or heavy cream into the soup. Season with salt and pepper, then ladle into ovenproof bowls. They should be about three-quarters full.

4. Lightly flour a surface, then roll out the pastry. Cut out circles or squares large enough to cover the tops of the bowls with a ½-inch overlap. Brush the rim of each bowl with water, lay the pastry on top, press around the rim, and pierce the centers. Bake in the preheated oven for 20–25 minutes, or until the pastry is golden. Serve immediately.

1
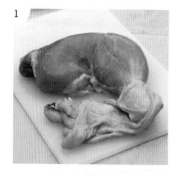

1

4

HEALTHY HINT
Of course, you could always remove the pastry to reduce the calories and swap to nonfat Greek yogurt for a lighter alternative.

Clam & Pasta Soup

 SERVES 6

 PREP TIME: 10 minutes

 COOKING TIME: 30–35 minutes

nutritional information per serving	212 cal, 6.5g fat, 1g sat fat, 6.5g total sugars, 0.8g salt

A great way to feed a hungry crowd using fresh clams when in season. Make sure you have some warm crusty bread standing by to mop up all the delicious flavors.

INGREDIENTS

3 tablespoons olive oil

1 Spanish onion, finely chopped

3 cloves garlic, finely chopped

2½ cups canned diced tomatoes

2 tablespoons tomato paste

2 teaspoons sugar

1 teaspoon dried oregano

4 cups vegetable stock

1 pound fresh clams, scrubbed

¾ cup dry white wine

3 ounces dried conchigliette

3 tablespoons chopped fresh flat-leaf parsley

salt and pepper, to taste

1. Heat the oil in a large saucepan. Add the onion and garlic and cook over low heat, stirring occasionally, for 5 minutes, until softened. Add the tomatoes, tomato paste, sugar, oregano, and stock and season with salt and pepper. Mix well and bring to a boil, then reduce the heat, cover, and simmer, stirring occasionally, for 5 minutes.

2. Discard any clams with broken shells and any that refuse to close when tapped. Put the clams into a saucepan, pour in the wine, cover, and cook over high heat, shaking the pan occasionally, for 3–5 minutes.

3. Remove the clams from the heat and remove from the liquid with a slotted spoon. Reserve the cooking liquid. Discard any clams that remain closed and remove the remainder from the half shells. Strain the reserved cooking liquid through a cheesecloth-lined strainer into a bowl and set aside.

4. Add the pasta to the soup and simmer, uncovered, for 10 minutes. Add the cooked clams and the reserved cooking liquid. Stir well and heat gently for 4–5 minutes; do not let the soup come back to a boil. Taste and adjust the seasoning, if necessary, stir in the parsley, and serve immediately.

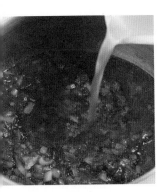

Roast Pumpkin, Garlic, & Thyme Soup

 SERVES 6   PREP TIME: 10 minutes   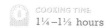 COOKING TIME: 1¼–1½ hours

nutritional information per serving	310 cal, 20g fat, 8g sat fat, 8.5g total sugars, 0.6g salt

Roasting the garlic bulbs brings out the sweetness and adds flavor to this classic soup with a twist.

INGREDIENTS

¼ cup olive oil, plus extra for drizzling

2 garlic bulbs

1 butternut squash or other winter squash (about 2 pounds)

2 tablespoons fresh thyme leaves, plus extra sprigs to garnish

2 tablespoons butter

1 onion, chopped

1 tablespoon all-purpose flour

5 cups chicken stock

½ cup crème fraîche or sour cream

salt and pepper, to taste

1. Preheat the oven to 375°F. Pour ½ tablespoon of the oil over each garlic bulb and season with salt and pepper, then wrap in aluminum foil and put in a large roasting pan. Peel and seed the squash, then cut the flesh into large chunks. Toss the squash in the remaining oil, season with salt and pepper, and sprinkle with half the thyme leaves. Put in the roasting pan in a single layer and cook in the preheated oven for 1 hour.

2. Melt the butter in a large saucepan. Add the onion and cook over medium heat, stirring occasionally, for 5 minutes, until soft. Stir in the flour and cook for 2 minutes. Add the stock, a few spoonfuls at a time to begin with, then add the remainder, stirring constantly.

3. When the squash has browned, remove the roasting pan from the oven. Add the squash to the saucepan and simmer for 10 minutes.

4. Open the garlic packages and let cool. When cool enough to handle, break up the garlic bulbs, put the cloves on a cutting board, and press down on each until the garlic pulp squeezes out.

5. Remove the soup from the heat and let cool slightly. Stir in the garlic pulp and the remaining thyme leaves, then transfer to a food processor or blender, in batches if necessary, and process until smooth. Return the soup to the rinsed-out pan and reheat gently; do not boil.

6. Ladle into warm bowls and top each with a spoonful of the crème fraîche or sour cream. Drizzle with a little oil, garnish with thyme sprigs, and serve immediately.

Russian Borscht

 SERVES 6   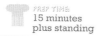 PREP TIME: 15 minutes plus standing    COOKING TIME: 1½–1¾ hours

nutritional information per serving	252 cal, 10g fat, 6g sat fat, 22g total sugars, 1.1g salt

This sweet-and-sour soup based on beet and tomatoes and flavored with a fresh bouquet garni is popular in many Eastern and central European countries. It can be served hot or cold.

INGREDIENTS

5 raw beets (about 2¼ pounds)
5 tablespoons butter
2 onions, thinly sliced
3 carrots, thinly sliced
3 celery stalks, thinly sliced
6 tomatoes, peeled, seeded, and chopped
1 tablespoon red wine vinegar
1 tablespoon sugar
2 cloves garlic, finely chopped
1 bouquet garni (3 fresh parsley sprigs, 2 fresh thyme sprigs, and 1 bay leaf, tied together)
5½ cups vegetable stock
salt and pepper, to taste
sour cream, to serve
chopped fresh dill, to garnish

1. Peel and shred four of the beets. Melt the butter in a large saucepan. Add the onions and cook over low heat, stirring occasionally, for 5 minutes, until softened. Add the shredded beets, carrots, and celery and cook, stirring occasionally, for an additional 5 minutes.

2. Increase the heat to medium, add the tomatoes, vinegar, sugar, garlic, and bouquet garni, season with salt and pepper, and stir well, then pour in the stock and bring to a boil. Reduce the heat, cover, and simmer for 1¼ hours.

3. Meanwhile, peel and shred the remaining beet. Add it and any juices to the pan and simmer for an additional 10 minutes. Remove the pan from the heat and let stand for 10 minutes.

4. Remove and discard the bouquet garni. Ladle the soup into warm bowls and top each with a spoonful of sour cream, sprinkle with chopped dill, and serve immediately.

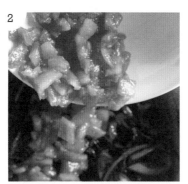

Miso Soup

 SERVES 2

 PREP TIME: 10 minutes

 COOKING TIME: 15–20 minutes

| nutritional information per serving | 154 cal, 7g fat, 0.8g sat fat, 1g total sugars, 2.7g salt |

Miso is a highly nutritious staple in Japan, made from fermented soybeans. Together with barley or rice, it adds a unique umami-base flavor.

INGREDIENTS

4 cups water

2 teaspoons dashi granules

6 ounces silken tofu, drained and cut into small cubes

4 shiitake mushrooms, finely sliced

4 tablespoons miso paste

2 scallions, chopped

1. Put the water in a large saucepan with the dashi granules and bring to a boil. Add the tofu and mushrooms, reduce the heat, and let simmer for 3 minutes.

2. Stir in the miso paste and let simmer gently, stirring, until the miso has dissolved.

3. Add the scallions and serve immediately. If you let the soup sit, the miso will settle, so give the soup a thorough stir before serving to recombine.

1

2
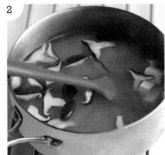

3

SOMETHING DIFFERENT

If you don't have shiitake mushrooms, use portobello mushrooms, which are more readily available.

Crab & Ginger Soup

 SERVES 4   PREP TIME: 10 minutes   COOKING TIME: 25–30 minutes

nutritional information per serving	363 cal, 16g fat, 5g sat fat, 6g total sugars, 1.7g salt

The rich crabmeat is offset perfectly by the aromatic ginger, sweet coconut milk, and fresh lime juice and rind, making a delicious Thai-inspired soup.

INGREDIENTS

2 tablespoons chili oil

1 clove garlic, chopped

4 scallions, trimmed and sliced

2 red bell peppers, seeded and chopped

1 tablespoon grated fresh ginger

4 cups fish stock

3½ cups coconut milk

½ cup rice wine or sherry

2 tablespoons lime juice

1 tablespoon grated lime rind

6 young kaffir lime leaves, finely shredded

10 ounces freshly cooked crabmeat

8 ounces freshly cooked crab claws

1 cup drained, canned corn kernels

1 tablespoon chopped fresh cilantro, plus a few sprigs to garnish

salt and pepper, to taste

1. Heat the oil in a large saucepan over medium heat. Add the garlic and scallions and cook, stirring, for about 3 minutes, until slightly softened. Add the red bell peppers and ginger and cook for an additional 4 minutes, stirring.

2. Pour in the stock and season with salt and pepper. Bring to a boil, then reduce the heat. Pour in the coconut milk, rice wine, and lime juice, and stir in the grated lime rind and kaffir lime leaves. Simmer for 15 minutes.

3. Add the crabmeat and crab claws to the soup with the corn and cilantro. Cook the soup for 5 minutes, or until the crab is heated through.

4. Remove from the heat. Ladle into warm soup bowls, garnish with sprigs of cilantro, and serve immediately.

Salmon Ramen Soup

 SERVES 4 PREP TIME: 10 minutes  COOKING TIME: 20–25 minutes

nutritional information per serving	500 cal, 19g fat, 3.5g sat fat, 5g total sugars, 2.9g salt

In this recipe, the salmon is broiled in a sweet sticky teriyaki marinade and served on a bowl of broth with egg noodles and Asian spices. It's warming, satisfying, and easy to prepare.

INGREDIENTS

4 cups vegetable stock
1 clove garlic
½ teaspoon light soy sauce
4 salmon fillets, about
5 ounces each, skinned
sunflower oil, for brushing
5 ounces dried ramen noodles
3½ cups baby spinach leaves
4 scallions, finely chopped

teriyaki glaze
2½ tablespoons sake
2½ tablespoons dark soy sauce
2 tablespoons mirin
or sweet sherry
1½ teaspoons packed light
brown sugar
½ clove garlic, minced
¼-inch piece fresh ginger, minced

to serve
1 cup fresh bean sprouts
1 fresh green chile,
seeded and sliced
fresh cilantro leaves

1. Preheat the broiler to high. Put the stock in a saucepan, add the garlic clove and soy sauce, and bring to a boil. Remove from the heat and set aside.

2. Mix together the ingredients for the teriyaki glaze and brush one surface of each salmon fillet with the glaze. Lightly brush the broiler rack with oil and cook the salmon under the preheated broiler for 4 minutes on only one side. The fish should be almost cooked through and flake easily. Remove from the broiler and set aside.

3. Meanwhile, cook the noodles in a saucepan of boiling water according to the package directions, until tender.

4. Remove the garlic from the stock, then bring the stock back to a boil. Drop in the spinach leaves and scallions and cook until the leaves are just wilted. Use a slotted spoon to remove the spinach and scallions from the pan and divide them among warm bowls. Divide the noodles among the bowls, then add a salmon fillet to each. Carefully pour the boiling stock into each bowl.

5. Sprinkle with the bean sprouts, chile, and cilantro leaves and serve immediately.

French Onion Soup

 SERVES 6

 PREP TIME:
30 minutes

 COOKING TIME:
1½ hours

nutritional information per serving : 480 cal, 23g fat, 11g sat fat, 7.5g total sugars, 2.2g salt

Traditionally, this is a soup served throughout the night to workers at the famous Les Halles market in Paris.

INGREDIENTS

6 onions (about 1½ pounds)

3 tablespoons olive oil

4 cloves garlic, 3 chopped and 1 kept whole

1 teaspoon sugar

2 teaspoons chopped fresh thyme, plus extra sprigs to garnish

2 tablespoons all-purpose flour

½ cup dry white wine

8½ cups vegetable stock

6 slices French bread

2½ cups shredded Gruyère cheese

1. Thinly slice the onions. Heat the oil in a large, heavy saucepan over medium–low heat, add the onions and cook, stirring occasionally, for 10 minutes, or until they are just beginning to brown. Stir in the chopped garlic, sugar, and chopped thyme, then reduce the heat and cook, stirring occasionally, for 30 minutes, or until the onions are golden brown.

2. Sprinkle in the flour and cook, stirring continuously, for 1–2 minutes. Stir in the wine. Gradually stir in the stock and bring to a boil, skimming off any foam that rises to the surface, then reduce the heat and simmer for 45 minutes. Meanwhile, preheat the broiler to medium–high. Toast the bread on both sides under the broiler, then rub the toast with the whole garlic clove.

3. Ladle the soup into six flameproof bowls set on a baking sheet. Float a piece of toast in each bowl and divide the shredded cheese among them. Place under the broiler for 2–3 minutes, or until the cheese has just melted. Garnish with thyme sprigs and serve at once.

1

2

3

SOMETHING
DIFFERENT
Try using red
onions for a
slightly sweeter,
milder flavor.

Vietnamese Crab Soup

 SERVES 6

 PREP TIME:
10 minutes
plus soaking

 COOKING TIME:
15–20 minutes

nutritional information per serving	288 cal, 11g fat, 1.5g sat fat, 1.5g total sugars, 2.6g salt

Light, clean, and fresh, this broth is quick and simple to make and perfect to kick off an Asian-style meal.

INGREDIENTS

6 dried shiitake mushrooms

1½ cups hot water

5 scallions

12 ounces asparagus spears, trimmed

1½ pounds white crabmeat, thawed if frozen

2 tablespoons peanut oil

3 cloves garlic, finely chopped

7 cups vegetable stock

1–2 tablespoons Thai fish sauce

3 tablespoons chopped fresh cilantro

1. Put the mushrooms into a bowl, pour in the water, and let soak for 20 minutes. Meanwhile, chop the white parts of the scallions and thinly slice the green parts diagonally. Slice the asparagus diagonally into ¾-inch pieces. Pick over the crabmeat and remove any pieces of shell and cartilage.

2. Drain the mushrooms, reserving the soaking liquid, and squeeze gently to remove the excess liquid. Remove and discard the stems and thinly slice the caps. Strain the soaking liquid through a cheesecloth-lined strainer.

3. Heat the oil in a large saucepan. Add the chopped scallions and garlic and stir-fry over medium heat for 2 minutes. Pour in the stock and reserved soaking liquid, add the mushrooms, and bring to a boil.

4. Stir in 1 tablespoon of the Thai fish sauce, add the sliced scallions and asparagus pieces, and bring back to a boil. Reduce the heat and simmer for 5 minutes, then gently stir in the crabmeat and cilantro. Simmer for an additional 3–4 minutes to heat through.

5. Remove the pan from the heat, taste, and stir in more fish sauce, if necessary. Ladle into warm bowls and serve immediately.

3

4

Mixed Bean Soup with Gruyère

 SERVES 4   PREP TIME: 15 minutes    COOKING TIME: 50–55 minutes

nutritional information
per serving   473 cal, 29g fat, 16g sat fat, 9g total sugars, 1.8g salt

Full of beans, vegetables, and fresh herbs and finished with tangy cheese, this is a satisfying soup.

INGREDIENTS

1 tablespoon olive oil
3 cloves garlic, finely chopped
4 scallions, sliced, plus extra to serve
3 cups sliced white mushrooms
4 cups vegetable stock
1 large carrot, chopped
2 cups rinsed and drained mixed beans, such as kidney beans, pinto beans, and chickpeas
1 (28-ounce) can diced tomatoes
1 tablespoon chopped fresh thyme
1 tablespoon chopped fresh oregano
1½ cups shredded Gruyère cheese or Swiss cheese
¼ cup heavy cream, plus extra to serve
salt and pepper, to taste

1. Heat the oil in a large saucepan over medium heat. Add the garlic and scallions and cook, stirring, for 3 minutes, until slightly softened. Add the mushrooms and cook, stirring, for an additional 2 minutes.

2. Stir in the stock, then add the carrot, beans, tomatoes, and herbs. Season with salt and pepper. Bring to a boil, then reduce the heat and simmer for 30 minutes.

3. Remove the soup from the heat and let cool slightly. Transfer to a food processor or blender, in batches if necessary, and process until smooth.

4. Return the soup to the rinsed-out pan and stir in the cheese. Cook for an additional 10 minutes, then stir in the cream. Cook for 5 minutes, then remove from the heat. Ladle into warm bowls, top each with a swirl of cream and with scallions. Serve immediately.

1

2

4

peas
  Beef & Barley Broth 48
  Lemon, Chicken & Rice Soup 20
  Pea Soup 12
  Split Pea & Ham Soup 72
  Summer Vegetable Soup 62
pesto 84
  Potato & Pesto Soup 84
  Roast Tomato & Pesto Soup 50
pork
  Wonton Soup 100
potatoes
  Beef & Barley Broth 48
  Broccoli Soup 40
  Carrot & Cilantro Soup 54
  Leek & Potato Soup 10
  New England Clam Chowder 80
  Potato & Pesto Soup 84
  Southwest Vegetable Soup 98
puff pastry
  Chicken & Mushroom Soup with
    Puff Pastry 106
pumpkin
  Roast Pumpkin, Garlic & Thyme
    Soup 110

rice
  Lemon, Chicken & Rice Soup 20
Roast Pumpkin, Garlic &
    Thyme Soup 110
Roast Sweet Potato & Garlic
    Soup 94
Roast Tomato & Pesto Soup 50
rosemary
  Ham & Lentil Soup 18
Rustic Bread, Basil & Tomato
    Soup 82

sage
  Turkey, Sage & Mushroom
    Soup 92
Salmon Ramen Soup 118
scallions
  Chicken & Chipotle Soup 30
  Mixed Bean Soup with
    Gruyère 124
128

Spicy Chicken Noodle Soup 34
Spicy Corn Chowder 28
shallots
  Avocado Soup with Guacamole
    Toasts 104
  Carrot & Parsnip Soup 22
  Pea Soup 12
shrimp
  Fishermen's Soup 14
  Wonton Soup 100
soups 4
  essential staples 5
Southwest Vegetable Soup 98
Spiced Winter Squash Soup 58
spices 5
  Spiced Chickpea & Spinach
    Soup 86
  Spicy Chicken Noodle Soup 34
  Spicy Corn Chowder 28
spinach
  Lemon, Chicken & Rice Soup 20
  Lentil & Spinach Soup 68
  Spiced Chickpea & Spinach
    Soup 86
  Summer Vegetable Soup 62
Split Pea & Ham Soup 72
squash
  Mixed Squash Soup 32
  Roast Sweet Potato & Garlic
Soup 94
  Spiced Winter Squash Soup 58
stock 5
Summer Vegetable Soup 62
sweet potatoes
  Roast Sweet Potato & Garlic
    Soup 94

tarragon
  Chicken Noodle Soup 42
teriyaki glaze 118
thyme
  Chunky Vegetable Soup 38
  Cream of Mushroom Soup 90
  Fishermen's Soup 14
  French Onion Soup 120
  Mixed Squash Soup 32

Roast Pumpkin, Garlic & Thyme
  Soup 110
tofu
  Miso Soup 114
  Spicy Corn Chowder 28
tomatoes
  Bell Pepper & Tomato Soup 64
  Chicken & Bean Soup 56
  Chile Chicken Soup 88
  Chunky Vegetable Soup 38
  Clam & Pasta Soup 108
  Fishermen's Soup 14
  Lentil & Spinach Soup 68
  Mediterranean Vegetable
    Soup 44
  Roast Tomato & Pesto Soup 50
  Russian Borscht 112
  Rustic Bread, Basil & Tomato
    Soup 82
  Spiced Chickpea & Spinach
    Soup 86
  Tomato & White Bean Soup 76
  Tomato Soup 8
  Turkey, Sage & Mushroom
    Soup 92
turnip
  Beef & Barley Broth 48

vegetables 5
  Chunky Vegetable Soup 38
  Mediterranean Vegetable
    Soup 44
  Southwest Vegetable Soup 98
Vietnamese Crab Soup 122

wine
  Fishermen's Soup 14
Wonton Soup 100

yogurt
  Lentil & Spinach Soup 68

zucchini
  Chunky Vegetable Soup 38
  Zucchini Soup 52

Index

apples
Carrot & Celery Soup 46
asparagus
Asparagus Soup 60
Summer Vegetable Soup 62
Vietnamese Crab Soup 122
avocados
Avocado Soup with Guacamole
Toasts 104
Chicken & Chipotle Soup 30
Chile Chicken Soup 88
Chilled Avocado Soup 16

bacon
Cabbage & Bacon Soup 26
New England Clam Chowder 80
Potato & Pesto Soup 84
barley
Beef & Barley Broth 48
basil
Mediterranean Vegetable
Soup 44
Rustic Bread, Basil & Tomato
Soup 82
Summer Vegetable Soup 62
Tomato Soup 8
bean sprouts
Salmon Ramen Soup 118
beans 5
Bean Soup 24
Chicken & Bean Soup 56
Minestrone Soup 74
Mixed Bean Soup with
Gruyère 124
Tomato & White Bean Soup 76
beef
Beef & Barley Broth 48
Meatball Soup 78
beets
Borscht 112
bell peppers
Bell Pepper & Tomato Soup 64
Chicken & Bean Soup 56
Mediterranean Vegetable
Soup 44
Minestrone Soup 74
Spicy Corn Chowder 28

bok choy
Spicy Chicken Noodle Soup 34
Borscht 112
bread
Avocado Soup with Guacamole
Toasts 104
French Onion Soup 120
Rustic Bread, Basil & Tomato
Soup 82
Broccoli Soup 40

cabbage
Beef & Barley Broth 48
Cabbage & Bacon Soup 26
Meatball Soup 78
Minestrone Soup 74
Southwest Vegetable Soup 98
canned ingredients 5
carrots
Carrot & Celery Soup 46
Carrot & Cilantro Soup 54
Carrot & Parsnip Soup 22
Chicken Noodle Soup 42
Chunky Vegetable Soup 38
Ham & Lentil Soup 18
Lentil & Spinach Soup 68
Mixed Squash Soup 32
Spicy Corn Chowder 28
Split Pea & Ham Soup 72
celery
Broccoli Soup 40
Cabbage & Bacon Soup 26
Carrot & Celery Soup 46
Carrot & Cilantro Soup 54
Fishermen's Soup 14
Ham & Lentil Soup 18
Mixed Squash Soup 32
Spicy Corn Chowder 28
Split Pea & Ham Soup 72
cheese
French Onion Soup 120
Meatball Soup 78
Minestrone Soup 74
Mixed Bean Soup with
Gruyère 124

Pea Soup 12
chervil
Carrot & Parsnip Soup 22
chicken
Chicken & Bean Soup 56
Chicken & Chipotle Soup 30
Chicken & Mushroom Soup with
Puff Pastry 106
Chicken Noodle Soup 42
Chile Chicken Soup 88
Lemon, Chicken & Rice Soup 20
Spicy Chicken Noodle Soup 34
Wonton Soup 100
chickpeas
Spiced Chickpea & Spinach
Soup 86
chiles
Chicken & Chipotle Soup 30
Chile Chicken Soup 88
Spiced Pumpkin Soup 58
Spicy Chicken Noodle Soup 34
chives
Chilled Avocado Soup 16
Jerusalem Artichoke Soup 70
Leek & Potato Soup 10
Chunky Vegetable Soup 38
cider
Chicken & Mushroom Soup with
Puff Pastry 106
cilantro
Carrot & Cilantro Soup 54
Chicken & Chipotle Soup 30
Spiced Pumpkin Soup 58
Spicy Corn Chowder 288
clams
Clam & Pasta Soup 108
New England Clam Chowder 80
corn
Chicken & Bean Soup 56
Crab & Ginger Soup 116
Southwest Vegetable Soup 98
Spicy Corn Chowder 28
crab
Crab & Ginger Soup 116
Vietnamese Crab Soup 122
cream

Asparagus Soup 60
Avocado Soup with Guacamole
  Toasts 104
Borscht 112
Carrot & Parsnip Soup 22
Chilled Avocado Soup 16
Cream of Mushroom Soup 90
Jerusalem Artichoke Soup 70
Leek & Potato Soup 10
Lobster Bisque 102
Mixed Bean Soup with
  Gruyère 124
New England Clam Chowder 80
Potato & Pesto Soup 84
Spiced Pumpkin Soup 58
Zucchini Soup 52
ème fraîche
Mixed Squash Soup 32
Pea Soup 12
Roasted Pumpkin, Garlic &
  Thyme Soup 110
Roasted Sweet Potato & Garlic
  Soup 94
croutons
Broccoli Soup 40
Jerusalem Artichoke Soup 70
Pea Soup 12

eggplants
Mediterranean Vegetable
  Soup 44

fish
Fishermen's Soup 14
Salmon Ramen Soup 118
flavorings 5
French Onion Soup 120

garlic
Bean Soup 24
Cabbage & Bacon Soup 26
Chicken & Bean Soup 56
Clam & Pasta Soup 108
Cream of Mushroom Soup 90
Minestrone Soup 74
Roasted Pumpkin, Garlic &
  Thyme Soup 110
Roasted Sweet Potato & Garlic
  Soup 94

Roasted Tomato & Pesto Soup 50
Rustic Bread, Basil & Tomato
  Soup 82
Summer Vegetable Soup 62
ginger
Crab & Ginger Soup 116
Spiced Pumpkin Soup 58
guacamole toasts 104

ham
Ham & Lentil Soup 18
Minestrone Soup 74
Split Pea & Ham Soup 72
herbs 5

Jerusalem Artichoke Soup 70

leeks
Beef & Barley Broth 48
Broccoli Soup 40
Leek & Potato Soup 10
Lemon, Chicken & Rice Soup 20
lentils
Ham & Lentil Soup 18
Lentil & Spinach Soup 68
limes
Chicken & Chipotle Soup 30
Crab & Ginger Soup 116
Lobster Bisque 102

Meatball Soup 78
Mediterranean Vegetable Soup 44
milk
Asparagus Soup 60
Carrot & Cilantro Soup 54
Minestrone Soup 74
mint dressing 86
miso
Miso Soup 114
Spicy Chicken Noodle Soup 34
Mixed Bean Soup with
  Gruyère 124
Mixed Squash Soup 32
mushrooms
Chicken & Mushroom Soup with
  Puff Pastry 106
Cream of Mushroom Soup 90

Miso Soup 114
Turkey & Mushroom Soup 92
Vietnamese Crab Soup 122

noodles 5
Chicken Noodle Soup 42
Salmon Ramen Soup 118
Spicy Chicken Noodle Soup 34

oils 5
olive oil
Jerusalem Artichoke Soup 70
Minestrone Soup 74
onions
Cabbage & Bacon Soup 26
Carrot & Cilantro Soup 54
Chunky Vegetable Soup 38
Fishermen's Soup 14
French Onion Soup 120
Ham & Lentil Soup 18
Mixed Squash Soup 32
Potato & Pesto Soup 84
Roasted Tomato & Pesto Soup 50
Split Pea & Ham Soup 72
Tomato & White Bean Soup 76
Zucchini Soup 52
oregano
Chile Chicken Soup 88
Mediterranean Vegetable
  Soup 44

parsley
Bean Soup 24
Cabbage & Bacon Soup 26
Chicken & Bean Soup 56
Chilled Avocado Soup 16
Fishermen's Soup 14
Lemon, Chicken & Rice Soup 20
parsnips
Carrot & Parsnip Soup 22
pasta 5
Bean Soup 24
Clam & Pasta Soup 108
Meatball Soup 78
Minestrone Soup 74
Potato & Pesto Soup 84

HEALTHY HINT

If you are watching calories and fat content, then swap the heavy cream for low-fat Greek yogurt and use just a sprinkling of Gruyère.